ASIA SMALL AND MEDIUM-SIZED ENTERPRISE MONITOR 2021

VOLUME II—HOW ASIA'S SMALL BUSINESSES SURVIVED A YEAR INTO THE COVID-19 PANDEMIC: SURVEY EVIDENCE

APRIL 2022

ASIAN DEVELOPMENT BANK

© 2022 Asian Development Bank
6 ADB Avenue, Mandaluyong City, 1550 Metro Manila, Philippines
Tel +63 2 8632 4444; Fax +63 2 8636 2444
www.adb.org

Some rights reserved. Published in 2022.

ISBN 978-92-9269-486-9 (print); 978-92-9269-487-6 (electronic); 978-92-9269-488-3 (ebook)
Publication Stock No. TCS220169-2
DOI: http://dx.doi.org/10.22617/TCS220169-2

Note:
In this publication, "B" refers to baht, "KN" to kip, and "$" refers to United States dollars.

Cover design by Claudette Rodrigo.

Contents

Tables, Figures, and Box

Foreword

Throughout the coronavirus disease (COVID-19) pandemic, governments, businesses, and people across Asia and the Pacific struggled to adjust to an ever-evolving new normal. Most countries took swift steps to contain the spread of infections through lockdowns, restrictions on mobility, social distancing and, once available, by establishing vaccine rollout programs. As the pandemic intensified, governments created comprehensive support packages for individuals, households, and businesses to minimize the effects of the restrictions on livelihoods and the availability of goods and services. These efforts set the stage for economic recovery. The Asian Development Bank (ADB) estimates that developing Asia rebounded from a 0.8% contraction in 2020 to 6.9% growth in 2021, and forecasts 5.2% growth in 2022. However, since early 2021, the appearance of variants—such as Delta and Omicron—created risk that new outbreaks would slow progress. Many countries have now started thinking of ways of living with a more endemic COVID-19.

Micro, small, and medium-sized enterprises (MSMEs) comprise over 90% of businesses in most countries in the region. Strengthening their development supports the goal of ensuring a sustainable and resilient recovery from the pandemic by boosting productivity and creating jobs. Thus, understanding how COVID-19 affected MSMEs helps build a foundation for better designing post-pandemic policies that effectively utilize national budgetary resources.

ADB's Economic Research and Regional Cooperation Department (ERCD) monitored how MSMEs survived their first year of the pandemic. It conducted surveys in Indonesia, the Lao People's Democratic Republic, the Philippines, and Thailand during March–April 2020 and March–April 2021—as part of the Asia Small and Medium-Sized Enterprise Monitor (ASM) project. These surveys were completed in partnership with leading government authorities and private sector groups.

Volume II of ASM 2021 offers insights on what approaches could work best to support a pandemic exit strategy and what policies may help revitalize the MSME sector during recovery in a way that creates a more resilient national economy. We expect this report to facilitate policy discussions on MSME pandemic-related assistance nationally, regionally, and globally.

Albert Park
Chief Economist and Director General
Economic Research and Regional Cooperation Department
Asian Development Bank

Acknowledgments

The Asia Small and Medium-Sized Enterprise Monitor (ASM) 2021 Volume II was prepared by Shigehiro Shinozaki, senior economist, Economic Research and Regional Cooperation Department (ERCD) of the Asian Development Bank (ADB). The work was supported by Satoru Yamadera from ERCD's financial cooperation and integration team. Key findings were discussed at an ERCD seminar held on 17 February 2022. It benefited from the advice and inputs from Albert Park, chief economist and director general of ERCD; and Joseph Ernest Zveglich Jr., deputy chief economist of ERCD.

The follow-up surveys on micro, small, and medium-sized enterprises (MSMEs) in Indonesia, the Lao People's Democratic Republic (Lao PDR), the Philippines, and Thailand were redesigned based on the first rapid survey conducted in March–April 2020, coordinated, and implemented by a special unit on business surveys under the ASM team, including Shigehiro Shinozaki as team leader and Josephine Penaflor Ferre, ADB consultant.

The online surveys were distributed in the four countries through (i) the Indonesian Chamber of Commerce and Industry and Ministry of Finance; (ii) the Department of SME Promotion of the Ministry of Industry and Commerce in the Lao PDR; (iii) the Bureau of Small and Medium Enterprise Development of the Department of Trade and Industry, and the Philippine Chamber of Commerce and Industry in the Philippines; and (iv) the Office of Small and Medium Enterprise Promotion, the Thai Credit Guarantee Corporation, and the Thai Chamber of Commerce in Thailand. The online surveys also used ADB Facebook pages, supported by the ADB Department of Communications, Indonesia Resident Mission, Lao PDR Resident Mission, the Philippines Country Office, and Thailand Resident Mission. For the March–April 2021 survey in Indonesia, the online survey was supplemented by field surveys conducted by the local survey firm Yayasan Akademika.

Shigehiro Shinozaki wrote the ASM 2021 Volume II. The special unit of business surveys led data processing. Administrative support was provided by Richard Supangan and Maria Frederika Bautista.

Abbreviations

ADB	—	Asian Development Bank
BPS	—	Badan Pusat Statistik (statistics office, Indonesia)
COVID-19	—	coronavirus disease
DERM	—	Department of Enterprise Registration and Management (Lao PDR)
GCQ	—	general community quarantine (Philippines)
GDP	—	gross domestic product
ECQ	—	enhanced community quarantine (Philippines)
Lao PDR	—	Lao People's Democratic Republic
MECQ	—	modified enhanced community quarantine (Philippines)
MSME	—	micro, small, and medium-sized enterprise
NCR	—	National Capital Region (Philippines)
NSO	—	National Statistical Office (Thailand)
PPKM	—	Pemberlakuan Pembatasan Kegiatan Masyarakat (Emergency Community Activity Restrictions) (Indonesia)
PSA	—	Philippine Statistics Authority (Philippines)
PSBB	—	Pembatasan Sosial Berskala Besar (Indonesia)

Executive Summary

From the start of the coronavirus disease (COVID-19) outbreak in early 2020, most countries in Asia and the Pacific reacted swiftly to contain the pandemic by imposing social restrictions and lockdowns. Governments worked quickly to provide emergency assistance for individuals, households, businesses, and their workers to minimize the impact of quarantines. As vaccines became available by the end of 2020, governments established vaccination rollout programs. Combined, these emergency health-care policies and economic stimulus laid the groundwork for businesses to reopen and economic recovery in many countries. However, several coronavirus variants—Delta, Omicron, and other acute variants—appeared since early 2021, creating new outbreaks in many countries across the region. Countries must now consider ways to live with an endemic COVID-19.

The continued development of micro, small, and medium-sized enterprises (MSMEs) is critical to boost national productivity, create jobs, and drive a sustainable and resilient recovery from the pandemic in developing Asia. Given the prolonged pandemic, it is essential that funding is available for government assistance to MSMEs on a regular basis. Innovation is needed to build effective long-term support for MSMEs. Knowing how MSMEs survived the first year of the pandemic is an important first step in designing a feasible framework for effective policies during the recovery period within the constraints of national budgets.

With this in mind, the Asian Development Bank (ADB) conducted a series of surveys during 2020 and 2021 to assess how COVID-19 affected MSMEs in several Asian countries—Indonesia, the Lao People's Democratic Republic (Lao PDR), the Philippines, and Thailand. These surveys showed the business environment for MSME improved somewhat, with many reopening their businesses into 2021, even as domestic demand for their products and services had not fully recovered as of March–April 2021. The COVID-19 crisis split MSMEs into two groups—those hit hardest by the pandemic and social restrictions, and the small fraction that benefited. Those that reported a better business environment were mostly those dealing with essential daily goods and services, including food and health-care products. Those hardest hit were typically producing nonessential goods and services. The two groups reported vastly different revenues, as the pandemic heightened inequality among MSMEs.

In general, MSME employment improved into 2021. Layoffs and wage cuts fell. Instead, employee working options expanded—from work-from-home (teleworking) to reduced working hours and granted leaves. MSMEs with good employment management gradually increased. Financial conditions also improved among MSMEs. Those without cash or available funds decreased, while there were more MSMEs reporting they had sufficient short-term cash or funds to maintain operations. Most MSMEs continued to rely on informal financing and their own funds during the first year of the pandemic. With support from government financial assistance, however, their access to bank credit improved sharply, increasing demand for greater government funding. During this period, digital financing was not a popular option for MSMEs.

The surveys allowed the breakdown of analysis into specific groups and sectors. For example, the prolonged pandemic and government mobility restrictions seriously affected tourism across countries. Thus, tourism-related MSMEs—restaurants, hotels, tourist agents, transportation services, and souvenir shops—faced a very harsh business environment during the first year of the pandemic. Many reported huge revenue losses despite government support, such as travel incentive programs. Only now, with greater containment of COVID-19, can tourism begin to recover.

During the chaotic first year of the pandemic, more digitally operated MSMEs started up or expanded, changing MSME operations from traditional personal-contact business to e-commerce. This digital transformation continues to accelerate under the new normal. However, digitally operated MSMEs were not always successful. There were two streams of business clusters—those that increased profits substantially and those that did not. Some of the reasons for those less profitable included limited demand for nonessential goods and services during social restrictions, weak business models without a strategy before starting, unfamiliarity with using technology for operations, and poor cost management during digitalization. Digital transformation is a priority for post-pandemic policies across countries. Given the limited use of digital financial services, even among digitally operated firms, any digitalization policy framework should be combined with promoting digital financial services that improve MSMEs internal cost management.

Women-led MSMEs—those owned or operated by women—showed mixed performance during the pandemic. They were also split into those hurt by the pandemic and those which benefited. Those reporting higher revenues were likely digitally operated. Like tourism-related MSMEs, internationalized MSMEs—those involved in the global supply chain or export/import business—faced a harsh business climate a year into the pandemic. They were directly affected by lockdowns and mobility restrictions, faced severe supply chain disruptions and had many contracts canceled. New digitalization policies should help foster women-led and internationalized MSMEs.

Finance was the top concern for MSMEs surveyed. They continued to struggle to reduce costs—including further layoffs—to continue operating. As COVID-19 becomes more endemic, cost management needs to become "smarter." Digitalizing MSME operations and administration is a potential solution for smart cost reduction. The surveys found that MSMEs expected further government support to access finance, subsidy programs, and tax relief. They also needed to be better informed about government assistance programs. Importantly, they want to strengthen business resilience against shocks, with government offering business development and advisory services along with skills training for workers.

The survey findings suggest MSME development policies should be well designed with a pandemic "exit" strategy in two stages: (i) policies based on living with COVID-19 and (ii) post-pandemic policies should it become endemic. "On-pandemic" MSME development policies include four strategic approaches: (i) provide timely information on government support programs; (ii) elaborate focus group assistance with proportionate measures; (iii) set a phased approach for assistance with defined budget allocations; and (iv) promote digital transformation and other technology for business. "Post-pandemic" MSME development policies also include four strategic approaches: (i) provide business development services and skills development training for workers; (ii) foster incubators and accelerators to encourage entrepreneurship; (iii) provide more growth capital by diversifying financing options; and (iv) use more private sector resources to implement policies. The post-pandemic policies can begin during the on-pandemic period as well. These need to focus more on the "growth" of MSMEs to boost national productivity and create more quality jobs—by enhancing the dynamism of MSMEs to ensure a sustainable and resilient pandemic recovery.

Given the urgency of understanding MSME conditions during the pandemic for policy design, the study used online surveys (nonstandard sampling procedures). As a result, respondents fell into different groups in respective data points (March–April 2020, August–September 2020, and March–April 2021). Nonetheless, it remains meaningful for the analysis to focus on changes of the respondents within the same group of MSMEs during 1 year into the pandemic. The analysis suggests that some MSMEs surveyed in 2020 might have gone out of business, while those more resilient to the effects of the pandemic appeared in 2021.

Introduction

There is increasing uncertainty over when, or even if, the coronavirus disease (COVID-19) will be contained. Over the 2 years of the pandemic thus far, people and businesses struggled to adjust their lives and business operations. In Asia and the Pacific, countries have shown good progress on nationwide vaccine rollouts, with many seeing a major reduction in COVID-19 infections. On the other hand, the appearance of new variants continues, heightening the risk of new outbreaks, which affects concerns among people and businesses that disease will become endemic.

Countries across the region responded rapidly to the initial shock, working to both contain the virus using various social restrictions and lockdowns while providing emergency assistance to individuals, households, businesses, and their workers. When vaccines became available after the first year, they rolled out vaccination programs, targeting the most vulnerable first. These emergency health-care investments and economic stimulus packages contributed to an economic recovery and business reopening in many countries. In developing Asia, gross domestic product (GDP) was estimated to have recovered from a 0.8% contraction in 2020 to 6.9% growth in 2021, and a forecast 5.2% in 2022.[1] For the surveyed countries in this study, the 2021 growth forecast was 3.7% in Indonesia (from −2.1% in 2020), 2.3% in the Lao People's Democratic Republic (Lao PDR) (from −0.5%), 5.6% in the Philippines (from −9.6%), and 1.6% in Thailand (from −6.2%). The continued appearance of new variants and recent global tensions are downside risks to 2022 growth estimates.

Micro, small, and medium-sized enterprises (MSMEs) play a critical role in boosting national productivity, creating jobs, and driving a more resilient growth across developing Asia. But they are less able to adapt to external shocks such as financial crises, climate change, and rapid changes in business climate such as the one brought about by the COVID-19 pandemic. As MSMEs will likely underpin a sustainable and resilient recovery from the pandemic, each country provided its own wide range of financial and nonfinancial policies to help MSMEs and their workers survive the pandemic, allotting huge amounts of their national budgets as support. This will continue until COVID-19 is finally contained or becomes endemic. Over the longer term, sizable funding will be needed to ensure sustainable assistance to MSMEs is available.

Understanding the impact of the pandemic on MSMEs creates a foundation for designing feasible post-pandemic policies within the confines of national budget capabilities. This report shows how Asia's small businesses survived 1 year into the pandemic and what policies could revitalize MSMEs. The Asian Development Bank (ADB) surveys were conducted in 2020–2021 to assess the change in impact of COVID-19 on MSMEs in Indonesia, the Lao PDR, the Philippines, and Thailand.

---

[1] ADB. 2022. *Asian Development Outlook 2022: Mobilizing Taxes for Development*. Manila.

Country Responses to COVID-19

Countries in Asia and the Pacific quickly employed several types of social restrictions—travel bans, school and business closures, restrictions on mobility, and social distancing—to contain the spread of COVID-19 from the beginning of the pandemic in March 2020. At the same time, they provided a wide range of emergency assistance measures—debt finance, tax relief, and subsidies—to help households, businesses, and their workers survive the first year of the pandemic. The countries surveyed in this study continue to provide comprehensive support for individuals and businesses, helping MSMEs and sectors virtually shut down, like tourism, with large government support. As of 15 November 2021, government support packages amounted to $115.3 billion (or 11.4% of 2020 GDP) in Indonesia, $41.6 million (0.2%) in the Lao PDR, $30.7 billion (8.7%) in the Philippines, and $105.8 billion (21.6%) in Thailand (ADB COVID-19 Policy Database).[2]

Indonesia put in place several large-scale social restrictions since 2020. In response to the first wave pandemic, the government adopted "Pembatasan Sosial Berskala Besar" (PSBB) in April–May 2020 and a second PSBB in September–November 2020, which included temporary business closures and mobility restrictions. In response to the second wave pandemic (Delta coronavirus variant), the government again imposed a partial mobility restrictions via the "Pemberlakuan Pembatasan Kegiatan Masyarakat" (PPKM; Emergency Community Activity Restrictions) in July–August 2021. These led to private businesses cutting back production and service delivery.

To ease the impact of social restrictions, the Government of Indonesia also launched several economic stimulus packages in 2020: (i) economic stimulus focusing on tourism in February; (ii) fiscal stimulus for tax relief in March; and (iii) the National Economic Recovery (PEN) program, covering financial and nonfinancial assistance for MSMEs. Financial assistance included an MSME credit guarantee program for working capital loans (6% until end-2020 and 3% until end-2021 with interest subsidies). The central bank provided liquidity support for banks to promote MSME lending, including capital injections to commercial banks and reduced policy rates. The government relaxed loan classifications and related procedures to help bank debt restructuring. Nonfinancial assistance included corporate income tax exemptions and discounts for MSMEs, with a wage subsidy program targeting 15.7 million workers, and a cash assistance program for micro and informal businesses (street vendors and stalls). These assistance measures were extended several times over the first year of the pandemic.

In the Lao PDR, the government imposed a nationwide lockdown in April–May 2020 in response to the first wave pandemic and a second lockdown in April–December 2021 to contain the second Delta variant wave with strict mobility restrictions and social distancing. Private businesses suspended operations during lockdowns. Export businesses and tourism were hit hardest. Food prices rose due to increased demand caused by the mobility restrictions. To support businesses and affected industries, the government and central bank implemented several assistance measures since the pandemic's first wave. For financial assistance, the central bank launched a special credit policy for MSMEs using an existing SME Promotion Fund. Through this fund, participating commercial banks offered concessional loans to MSMEs (5.5%–10.0% annual lending rate with interest subsidy; loan tenor up to

---

2   ADB COVID-19 Policy Database. https://covid19policy.adb.org/.

10 years). The central bank instructed commercial banks to defer loan repayments and promote debt restructuring and new loans under the credit policy. For nonfinancial assistance, the government offered income tax exemptions for employees of private businesses (with KN5 million per month) and profit tax exemptions for microenterprises (with annual incomes of KN50 million–KN400 million) for April–June 2021.

The Philippines had one of the longest lockdowns in the world. The government introduced its strictest lockdown—the enhanced community quarantine (ECQ)—in the National Capital Region (NCR) and neighboring provinces from mid-March to end-May 2020, imposing strict mobility restrictions, school and business closures, and social distancing. Depending on the number of COVID-19 cases, the government set different levels of lockdowns by area—ECQ, modified ECQ (MECQ), and general community quarantine (GCQ). To contain the second wave, the NCR and neighboring provinces were on ECQ again from late-March to end-April 2021, and the ECQ was again in force due to surging coronavirus cases in January 2022.

To help households and businesses weather the lockdowns, the Government of the Philippines promptly enacted the *Bayanihan* Act "Bayanihan to Heal as One Act" (*Bayanihan* means mutual cooperation) in March 2020, providing a mandatory grace period (30 days) for all loans by designated banks and nonbank finance institutions, including MSME loans. When expired in June 2020, a second *Bayanihan* Act "Bayanihan to Recover as One Act" became effective in September 2020 until end-2020, extending the grace period to 60 days. The central bank launched several regulations to facilitate commercial banks and nonbank finance institutions finance individuals and businesses, especially MSMEs and the worst-hit industries like tourism. These included policy rate cuts, eased compliance with the reserve requirements, and reduced credit risk weights for MSME loans. For MSME loans guaranteed by the Philippine Guarantee Corporation (PhilGuarantee), the credit risk weight was 0%. The guaranteed MSME loans were extended into 2021, with additional equity injections to PhilGuarantee. The government provided interest rate subsidies to extend MSME loans. The Department of Trade and Industry and the Department of Agriculture offered their own MSME loan programs for business development training and agribusiness. For nonfinancial assistance, the government also provided an emergency subsidy program, including wage subsidies, to employees of small businesses and cash-for-work programs for displaced workers. The lockdowns led to huge economic losses in the country, but a series of economic stimulus packages contributed to economic recovery.

In Thailand, the government announced a state of emergency in March 2020, imposing night curfews, prohibiting mass gatherings, several mobility restrictions, and lockdowns. The state of emergency was extended several times during the first year of the pandemic. Private businesses suspended or limited operations during lockdowns, seriously damaging the economy. In parallel, the government launched large-scale stimulus packages, including several assistance measures for MSMEs. Under the Emergency Decree of April 2020, the central bank provided liquidity support for financial institutions (commercial banks and specialized financial institutions) to offer concessional loans to MSMEs (existing borrowers) at a 2% annual lending rate for the first 2 years with credit lines not exceeding B500 million. The credit limit was set to 20% of the existing debt outstanding. The Ministry of Finance established a loss compensation scheme for up to 60%–70% of additional provisioning required and subsidized interest payments. Deferred debt repayment was available for MSME loans with credit lines not exceeding B100 million. The central bank also encouraged financial institutions to expedite debt restructuring for MSMEs. In 2021, a 10-year credit guarantee facility provided by the Thai Credit Guarantee Corporation—covering credit losses up to 40% of the portfolio—enabled MSMEs, both existing and new borrowers, to access soft loans at an average 5% annual lending rate for the first 5 years. Nonfinancial assistance included wage subsidies to employees of MSMEs to prevent mass layoffs (50% salary payouts covered) and cash handouts to self-employed and laid-off workers (B5,000 monthly).

Given the increased uncertainty of containing COVID-19 as new variants emerged, governments face the risk of further bloating national budget deficits to continue assistance programs to households, businesses, and their workers. In particular, extended financial assistance poses the risk of deteriorating financial institution balance sheets without continued government liquidity support. To what extent did government support help MSMEs and their workers a year into the pandemic? What policy options should be maintained, strengthened, or replaced during and after pandemic? What would be the best way to manage national budgets and allocate funds for assistance programs to MSMEs, hard-hit industrial sectors, and workers? What innovative ideas would ensure effective long-term support for MSMEs during and after the pandemic? To answer these questions, it is critical to understand the real conditions of MSMEs and their business operations and internal management. This is precisely what this study analyzes.

Methodology

To assess the COVID-19 impact on MSMEs 1 year into the pandemic, surveys were conducted three times in four countries—Indonesia, the Lao PDR, the Philippines, and Thailand. The surveys covered three data points: March–April 2020, August–September 2020, and March–April 2021. Due to the urgency of understanding how MSMEs were coping with the pandemic to help countries design the most appropriate policies, the study used online surveys. Samples were collected using networks of survey partners that monitor MSMEs nationwide. These survey partners included (i) the Indonesian Chamber of Commerce and Industry and the Ministry of Finance in Indonesia; (ii) the Department of SME Promotion of the Ministry of Industry and Commerce in the Lao PDR; (iii) the Bureau of Small and Medium Enterprise Development of the Department of Trade and Industry and the Philippine Chamber of Commerce and Industry in the Philippines; and (iv) the Office of Small and Medium Enterprise Promotion, the Thai Credit Guarantee Corporation, and the Thai Chamber of Commerce in Thailand. The online surveys also used ADB Facebook pages for the four countries. For the March–April 2021 survey in Indonesia, the online survey was supplemented by field surveys conducted by a local survey firm using enumerators.

The same set of survey questionnaires was used to compare the pandemic impact across data points. They had four components: (i) a company profile including its industry, location, operating period, ownership, employment, digital penetration (use of the internet for daily business or e-commerce), and global business exposure; (ii) business conditions that covered the business climate (environment), revenue, employment, wage payments, and financial conditions; (iii) business issues and concerns brought on by the pandemic; and (iv) policy measures MSMEs wanted to see to maintain business operations.[3]

Classifying MSMEs for analysis used national definitions (employment thresholds). For Indonesia, the definition was set by the Badan Pusat Statistik (BPS; statistics office): (i) 1–4 employees for micro, (ii) 5–19 for small, and (iii) 20–99 for medium-sized firms. For the Lao PDR, MSME categories were based on Decree No.25/GOL/2017: (i) 1–5 employees for micro, (ii) 6–50 for small, and (iii) 51–99 for medium-sized firms. For the Philippines, the definition was set by the Philippine Statistics Authority (PSA): (i) 1–9 employees for micro, (ii) 10–99 for small, and (iii) 100–199 for medium-sized firms. And for Thailand, MSME classification followed the Office of Small and Medium Enterprise Promotion definition introduced in November 2019: (i) 1–5 employees for micro, (ii) 6–30 for small services and trading firms and 6–50 for small manufacturing firms, and (iii) 31–100 for medium services and trading firms with 51–200 employees for medium manufacturing firms.

This report provides descriptive analysis based on unweighted data. Due to the lack of data needed for weighting adjustments—especially detailed distribution of establishments by size and industrial sector in national statistics such as the Lao PDR and Indonesia—we used unweighted data. But the samples were compared by size, sector, and region with available national statistics to understand possible data bias.

---

[3] The questionnaire used in the first rapid surveys in March–April 2020 was upgraded in the August–September 2020 and March–April 2021 surveys. Key components remained the same across the three data points, but the selection items in some questions were slightly modified for more detailed analysis in the second and third surveys.

Data Structure

The surveys collected a total of 3,831 valid samples from MSMEs in March–April 2020; 1,339 in August–September 2020; and 5,112 in March–April 2021 (Table 1). For Indonesia, the surveys received 525 completed MSME responses in March–April 2020; 128 in August–September 2020; and 2,509 in March–April 2021. For the Lao PDR, we received 355 in March–April 2020, just 5 in August–September 2020, and 94 in March–April 2021.[4] For the Philippines, it was 1,804 for March–April 2020; 686 in August–September 2020; and 1,546 in March–April 2021. For Thailand, 1,147 were collected in March–April 2020; 520 in August–September 2020; and 963 in March–April 2021. The second survey for August–September 2020 had lower samples mainly due to more immediate issues faced by MSMEs.

We tried to follow up frequently with all prior respondents throughout the year of the surveys through our survey partners, using phone contacts (the Lao PDR) and field interviews (Indonesia). But repeat respondents over the three survey periods were small—ranging from just 1.2% of the March–April 2021 survey in Indonesia to 11.7% in Thailand (Table 1). Besides MSMEs' survey fatigue, field interviews in Indonesia found that many MSMEs we initially surveyed had already closed, could not reopen their business due to positive COVID-19 tests, or some MSME owners passed away due to COVID-19. Thus, survey respondents formed different groups across the respective data points. Nonetheless, it is helpful in the analysis to focus on the change in respondents within the same group of MSMEs during 1 year into the pandemic.

Table 1: Total Number of MSME Respondents, 2020–2021

Country	March–April 2020	August–September 2020	March–April 2021	Repeated Respondents	Share to March–April 2021 (%)
Indonesia	525	128	2,509	31	1.2
Lao PDR	355	5	94	5	5.3
Philippines	1,804	686	1,546	27	1.7
Thailand	1,147	520	963	113	11.7
Total	3,831	1,339	5,112	176	5.0 (average)

Lao PDR = Lao People's Democratic Republic; MSME = micro, small, and medium-sized enterprise.
Source: Calculated based on data from ADB MSME surveys in Indonesia, the Lao PDR, the Philippines, and Thailand, March–April 2020, August–September 2020, and March–April 2021.

As we used online surveys, samples were not randomly selected and did not follow existing frameworks of national statistics; thus, the study adopted nonstandard sampling procedures. The rapid surveys using online platforms were prioritized to help governments design timely evidence-based policy support to MSMEs during the pandemic. It should be noted that online surveys face an issue of self-selection and nonresponse bias in survey data. To verify the extent of this bias, survey data were compared with the distribution of enterprise data provided by existing national statistics (Table 2 and Appendix 1).

---

[4]   For the August–September 2020 survey in the Lao PDR, the ADB survey had a conflict with the MSME surveys conducted by other organizations, where our survey partner Department of SME Promotion handled these surveys and physically could not handle our survey.

In Indonesia, as compared with the BPS 2016 Economic Census, micro and small firms were underrepresented by 1.6 percentage points for the March–April 2020 survey, 0.4 for the August–September 2020 survey, and 0.6 for the March–April 2021 survey.[5] By sector, the gap of percentage shares between the ADB surveys and the BPS census was around 4 percentage points in the first and second surveys and 5 percentage points in the third survey, with some exceptions (underrepresentation in manufacturing and trade, and overrepresentation in accommodation and other services). By region, the gap was around 5 percentage points in the first, 3 in the second, and 4 in the third survey with some exceptions.

In the Lao PDR, as compared with the enterprise database compiled by the Department of Enterprise Registration and Management (DERM) of the Ministry of Industry and Commerce as of 3 June 2020, MSMEs by sector had a gap of around 4 percentage points in the March–April 2020 survey and 6 percentage points in the March–April 2021 survey, with some exceptions (underrepresentation in trade and overrepresentation in accommodation and other services). By region, the gap was around 5 percentage points in the first and third surveys with some exceptions (overrepresentation in the capital region, Vientiane prefecture). Due to only five respondents in the August–September survey, the analysis for the Lao PDR for this period was removed from this report. As there were no statistical data by firm size, only aggregate MSME data by sector and region were comparable.

In the Philippines, against the PSA 2018 List of Establishments, microenterprises were underrepresented by 7.9 percentage points for the March–April 2020 survey, slightly overrepresented by 0.5 percentage point for the August–September 2020 survey, and underrepresented by 1.1 percentage points for the March–April 2021 survey. Small firms were overrepresented by 7.0 percentage points in the first survey, underrepresented by 1.3 percentage points in the second, and slightly overrepresented by 0.3 percentage point in the third survey. Medium-sized firms were overrepresented by 0.9 percentage point in the first and 0.8 percentage point in the second and third surveys. By sector, the gap between the survey data and the PSA list was around 5 percentage points in the first and second surveys and 4 percentage points in the third survey, with some exceptions (overrepresentation in manufacturing and underrepresentation in trade). By region, the gap was around 5 percentage points across the three surveys with some exceptions.

In Thailand, as compared with the National Statistical Office (NSO) 2017 Industrial Census, microenterprises were underrepresented by 29.9 percentage points for the March–April 2020 survey, 40.5 percentage points for the August–September 2020 survey, and 23.4 percentage points for the March–April 2021 survey. Small firms were overrepresented by 24.0 percentage points in the first survey, 33.6 percentage points in the second survey, and 20.8 percentage points in the third survey. Medium-sized firms were overrepresented by 5.9 percentage points in the first survey, 6.8 percentage points in the second, and 2.6 percentage points in the third. By sector, the gap between survey data and the NSO census was around 5 percentage points across the three surveys, with some exceptions (overrepresentation in manufacturing and underrepresentation in trade). By region, the gap was around 1 percentage point across the three surveys with the exception of overrepresentation by 9–20 percentage points in Bangkok.

Overall, in comparing ADB survey data with the national statistics distribution of establishments, the gap between percentage shares were not so large—around +/-5 percentage points—except firm size distribution in Thailand and some exceptions by sector and regions. Each sample group is considered at comparable levels.

---

[5]   BPS statistics have two categories by non-agriculture firm size: (i) micro and small firms and (ii) medium-sized and large firms.

Table 2: Comparison between ADB Surveys and National Statistics Distribution

Item		March–April 2020		August–September 2020		March–April 2021		Reference
		Gap	Remarks/Exceptions	Gap	Remarks/Exceptions	Gap	Remarks/Exceptions	
INO	By firm size	−1.6	Micro and small	−0.4	Micro and small	−0.6	Micro and small	BPS 2016 Economic Census
		+1.6	Medium and large	+0.4	Medium and large	+0.6	Medium and large	
	By sector	+/−4	Manufacturing -9.7	+/−4	Trade -23.1; manufacturing -6.2; accommodation +14.2; other services +12.0; professional services +7.2	+/−5	Manufacturing -13.7; trade -13.2; arts +14.9; accommodation +11.5; human health +11.5	
	By region	+/−5	Yogyakarta +5.5	+/−3	East Java +19.6; Cental Java −4.5	+/−4	Central Java -14.1; North Sumatra +17.4; West Java +16.9; Jakarta +7.3	
LAO	By firm size	n/a,		...	...	n/a,		DERM Enterprise Database, June 2020
	By sector	+/−5	Trade -19.1; transport -9.9; public admin +7.2; accommodation +6.7; admin +6.2			+/−4	Transport -13.3; finance +12.9; other services +10.0	
	By region	+/−4	Vientiane prefecture +16.0; Phongsali +7.4			+/−6	Vientiane prefecture +31.7	
PHI	By firm size	−7.9	Micro	+0.5	Micro	−1.1	Micro	PSA List of Establishment, 2018
		+7.0	Small	−1.3	Small	+0.3	Small	
		+0.9	Medium	+0.8	Medium	+0.8	Medium	
	By sector	+/−5	Manufacturig +20.0; trade -21.2	+/−5	Trade -24.3; manufacturing +15.7; agriculture +5.8; other services +5.2	+/−4	Trade -12.2; manufacturing +10.8; agriculture +6.2; other services +6.0	
	By region	+/−5	CALABARZON +10.2	+/−5	CALABARZON -12.5; Central Luzon -9.6; NCR -9.4; Central Visayas -6.2; Eastern Visayas +57.2; Ilocos +7.0	+/−5	NCR -12.6; CALABARZON -9.0; Cagayan valley +27.4; Zamboanga Peninsula +8.5	
THA	By firm size	−29.9	Micro	−40.5	Micro	−23.4	Micro	NSO 2017 Industrial Census Listing
		+24.0	Small	+33.6	Small	+20.8	Small	
		+5.9	Medium	+6.8	Medium	+2.6	Medium	
	By sector	+/−5	Trade -9.4; other services -9.0; accommodation -7.6; manufacturing +6.8; admin +6.4	+/−5	Trade -36.8; manufacturing +8.1; not identified +32.3	+/−5	Trade -21.7; accommodation -7.5; manufacturing +8.0	
	By region	+/−1 (mostly)	Bangkok +9.0	+/−1 (mostly)	Bangkok +12.5	+/−1 (mostly)	Bangkok +20.6	

ADB = Asian Development Bank, BPS = Badan Pusat Statistik, DERM = Department of Enterprise Registration and Management, INO = Indonesia, LAO = Lao People's Democratic Republic (Lao PDR), NCR = National Capital Region, NSO = National Statistical Office, PHI = Philippines, PSA = Philippine Statistics Authority, THA = Thailand.

Source: Calculated based on data from ADB MSME surveys in Indonesia, the Lao PDR, the Philippines, and Thailand, March–April 2020, August–September 2020, and March–April 2021.

Company Profiles

As mentioned earlier, each sample survey group was different. But the characteristics of surveyed MSMEs were considered homogeneous across observed countries and time series (Table 3). The majority of samples were microenterprises (51%–95% of the MSME respondents), followed by small (5%–40%) and medium-sized enterprises (1%–10%). They were mainly engaged in services (60%–94%), especially distributive trade, accommodation, and food services, followed by manufacturing (2%–35%) and agriculture (3%–10%). Samples were collected nationwide, although respondents were somewhat concentrated in capital cities and urban areas. Regional distribution maps are in Appendix 2.

Breaking down the survey data into specific groups, there were MSMEs engaged in tourism (4%–19% in Indonesia, 17%–19% in the Lao PDR, 4%–6% in the Philippines, and 8%–15% in Thailand).[6] Many of the MSMEs surveyed were young enterprises operating for up to 5 years (48%–61% in Indonesia, 43%–56% in the Lao PDR, 59%–65% in the Philippines, 26%–48% in Thailand). Around half or less were led by women (30%–50% in Indonesia, 46%–55% in the Lao PDR, 56%–63% in the Philippines, 39%–44% in Thailand). MSMEs involved in global supply chains or export/import business were a small fraction, except in Thailand (2%–6% in Indonesia, 8%–17% in the Lao PDR, 3%–10% in the Philippines, 30%–33% in Thailand). A relatively large share of MSMEs used the internet for daily business or engaged in online selling or e-commerce (28%–71% in Indonesia, 76%–78% in the Lao PDR, 35%–74% in the Philippines, 53%–96% in Thailand).[7]

As the survey samples were not sufficient for detailed analyses using unweighted data by firm size and industrial sector, this report focuses on aggregate MSME data to assess their impact during the first year of the pandemic.

Table 3: Profile of MSMEs Surveyed

Item		March–April 2020				August–September 2020			March–April 2021			
		INO	LAO	PHI	THA	INO	PHI	THA	INO	LAO	PHI	THA
Firm size (%)	Micro	79.8	58.0	81.0	60.7	94.5	89.4	67.5	89.4	51.1	87.8	50.6
	Small	17.1	38.6	17.6	33.7	4.7	9.3	27.7	8.7	40.4	10.9	39.5
	Medium	3.1	3.4	1.4	5.7	0.8	1.3	4.8	1.9	8.5	1.3	10.0
Industrial sector (%)	Agriculture	9.0	7.9	5.6	2.6	10.2	6.1	4.6	3.0	3.2	7.1	5.0
	Manufacturing	10.9	18.0	34.8	27.8	1.6	26.7	27.5	3.2	8.5	23.2	26.8
	Services	80.2	74.1	59.7	69.6	88.3	67.2	67.9	93.9	88.3	69.8	68.2

continued on next page

---

[6] Categorizing tourism in the first survey (March–April 2020) differed from the second (August–September 2020) and third (March–April 2021) surveys. The first survey used a reclassification of industrial sectors, while the second and third surveys used the self-declaration of membership with tourism organizations or associations.

[7] Data refer to respondents using the internet for daily business in the March–April 2020 survey and those engaged in online selling or e-commerce for the August–September 2020 and March–April 2021 surveys.

Table 3   *continued*

Item	March–April 2020				August–September 2020			March–April 2021			
	INO	LAO	PHI	THA	INO	PHI	THA	INO	LAO	PHI	THA
Specific groups											
Tourism industry (%)	4.4	18.6	6.4	8.1	18.8	4.4	14.8	6.2	17.0	4.1	12.3
Young-aged firms (up to 5y) (%)	49.9	43.4	59.2	45.8	60.9	59.8	47.5	47.5	56.4	65.3	25.7
Women-led MSMEs (%)	29.7	45.9	55.7	43.8	47.7	61.5	43.9	49.8	55.3	62.6	39.4
Internationalized MSMEs (%)	5.5	16.6	10.1	29.6	3.9	2.6	28.1	1.7	7.5	7.5	33.0
Digitally operated MSMEs (%)	71.4	77.8	74.2	95.6	59.4	45.7	62.9	28.1	75.5	34.8	53.3
Total MSME Respondents (number)	525	355	1,804	1,147	128	686	520	2,509	94	1,546	963

INO = Indonesia; LAO = Lao People's Democratic Republic (Lao PDR); MSME = micro, small, and medium-sized enterprise; PHI = Philippines; THA = Thailand.

Source: Calculated based on data from ADB MSME surveys in Indonesia, the Lao PDR, the Philippines, and Thailand, March–April 2020, August–September 2020, and March–April 2021.

The COVID-19 Impact on MSMEs during the First Year of the Pandemic

1. Business Environment

One year after the pandemic was announced on 11 March 2020, the business environment for MSMEs had improved moderately. In March–April 2020, half or more MSMEs suspended operations soon after the pandemic started due to mobility restrictions (48.6% of surveyed MSMEs in Indonesia, 61.1% in the Lao PDR, 70.6% in the Philippines, and 41.1% in Thailand) (Figure 1). In the same period of 2021, the share of MSMEs that were temporarily closed fell into single digits (4.8% in Indonesia, 1.1% in the Lao PDR, 6.3% in the Philippines, and 7.4% in Thailand). Many MSMEs had reopened. Statistics show the surveyed economies began recovering in 2021 (with growth projections of 1.6%–5.6% in 2021 from contractions of 0.5%–9.6% in 2020), which helped MSMEs reopen as well (footnote 1).

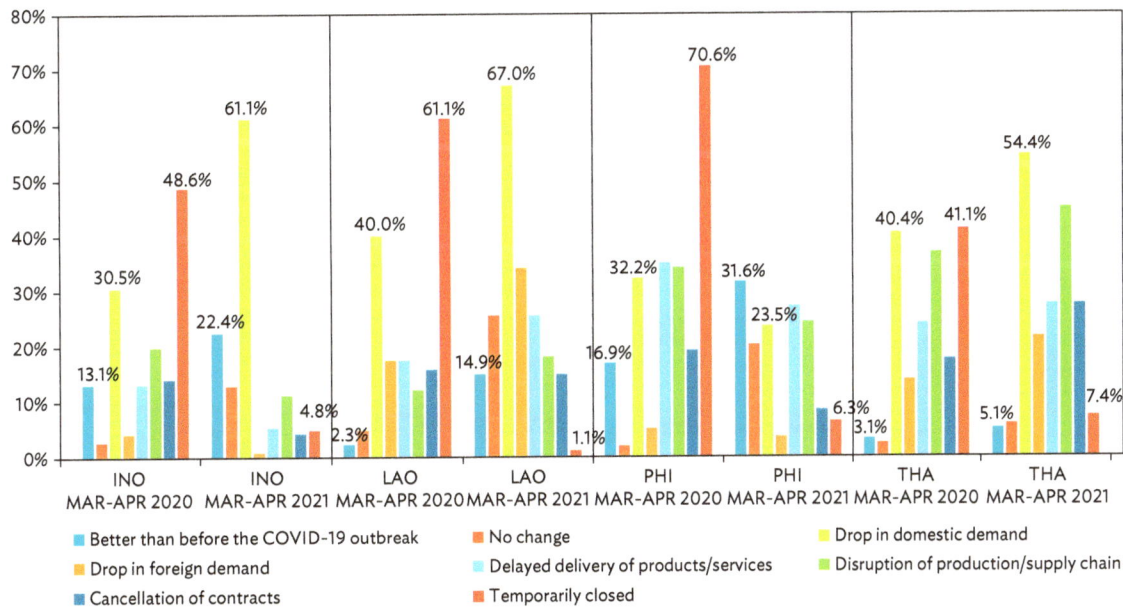

Figure 1: MSME Business Environment, 2020–2021

COVID-19 = coronavirus disease; INO = Indonesia; LAO = Lao People's Democratic Republic (Lao PDR); MSME = micro, small, and medium-sized enterprise; PHI = Philippines; THA = Thailand..

Note: For INO, 525 valid samples in March–April 2020 and 2,509 in March–April 2021; For LAO, 355 valid samples in March–April 2020 and 94 in March–April 2021; For PHI, 1,804 valid samples in March–April 2020 and 1,546 in March–April 2021; For THA, 1,147 valid samples in March–April 2020 and 963 in March–April 2021.

Source: Calculated based on MSME surveys in Indonesia, the Lao PDR, the Philippines, and Thailand, March–April 2020–2021.

However, there remained downside risks and continued uncertainty as pandemic remained entrenched. The drop in domestic demand for MSME products and services was likely to grow further based on surveys conducted in the following countries for 2020 and 2021: from 30.5% to 61.1% in Indonesia, from 40.0% to 67.0% in the Lao PDR, and from 40.4% to 54.4% in Thailand. For the Philippines, it fell somewhat from 32.2% to 23.5%. Meanwhile, there were MSMEs reporting a better business environment than before the outbreak, especially for retail services, mostly due to high demand for essential daily goods and services, including food and healthcare products (from 13.1% to 22.4% in 2021 in Indonesia, from 2.3% to 14.9% in the Lao PDR, from 16.9% to 31.6% in the Philippines, and from 3.1% to 5.1% in Thailand).

When interpreting the results, it should be noted that some MSMEs surveyed in 2020 had gone out of business by 2021, with those more resilient to the pandemic impact appearing in 2021 data, given the small share of respondents appearing in all surveys (Table 1).

2.   Impact on Revenue

MSME sales and revenue fell sharply in March 2020 and dropped further in April 2020 due to many business closures backed by mobility restrictions in observed countries (zero-revenue firms: 36.0% of MSMEs in March to 48.8% in April in Indonesia, 35.5% to 62.8% in the Lao PDR, 58.8% in March in the Philippines, and 27.2% in March to 38.9% in April in Thailand) (Figure 2).[8] This largely improved in March–April 2021, ranging from 2% to 9% across the countries surveyed (5.1% in Indonesia, 2.1% in the Lao PDR, 8.9% in the Philippines, and 8.8% in Thailand).

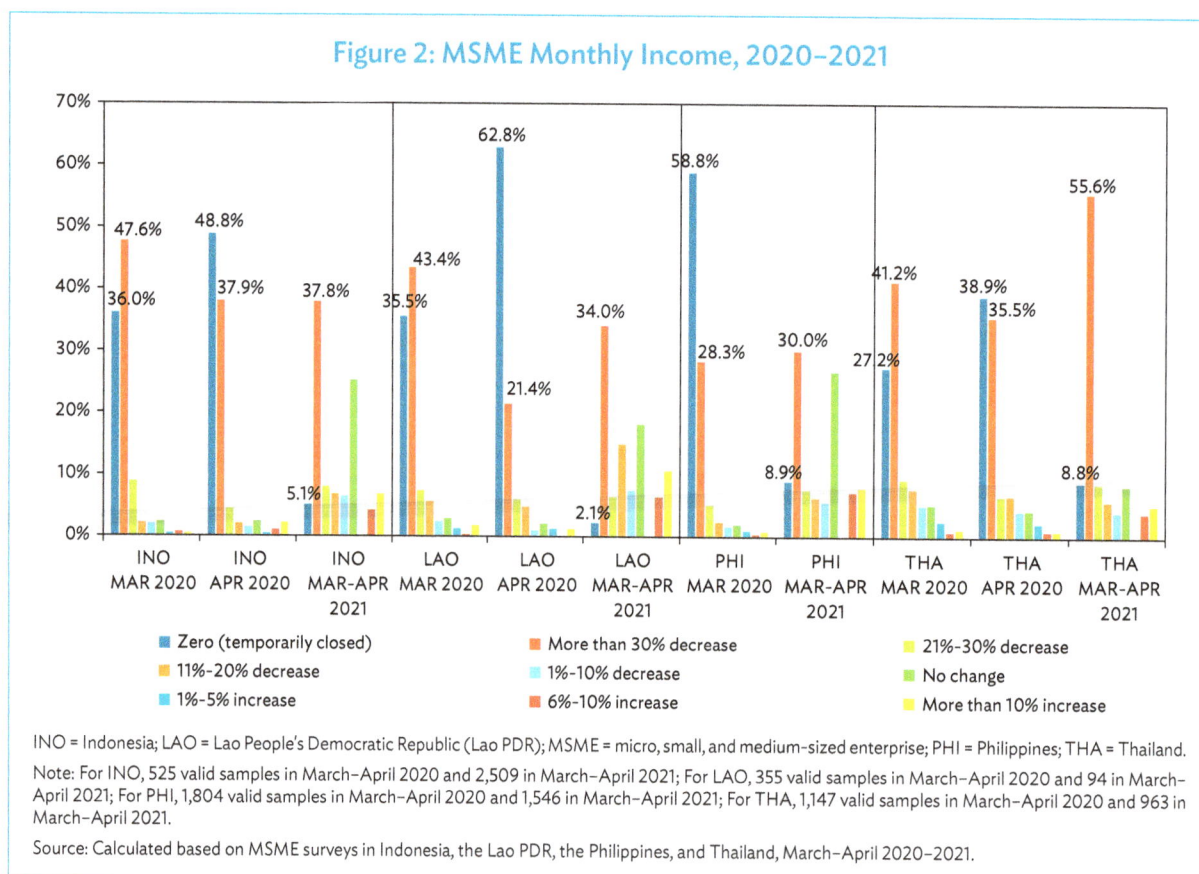

Figure 2: MSME Monthly Income, 2020–2021

INO = Indonesia; LAO = Lao People's Democratic Republic (Lao PDR); MSME = micro, small, and medium-sized enterprise; PHI = Philippines; THA = Thailand.

Note: For INO, 525 valid samples in March–April 2020 and 2,509 in March–April 2021; For LAO, 355 valid samples in March–April 2020 and 94 in March–April 2021; For PHI, 1,804 valid samples in March–April 2020 and 1,546 in March–April 2021; For THA, 1,147 valid samples in March–April 2020 and 963 in March–April 2021.

Source: Calculated based on MSME surveys in Indonesia, the Lao PDR, the Philippines, and Thailand, March–April 2020–2021.

---

8   For the Philippines, the question on revenue for April 2020 was not included in the March–April 2020 survey.

There was a shift in the sample groups from those severely affected in 2020 to those more resilient to shocks in 2021. However, around 30%–56% of MSMEs continued to face more than a 30% drop in revenue as of March–April 2021, particularly in Thailand (37.8% in Indonesia, 34.0% in the Lao PDR, 30.0% in the Philippines, and 55.6% in Thailand). A trickle-down effect from the economic recovery had not yet occurred for MSMEs at the time of the survey. A series of lockdowns and frequent mobility restrictions continued to hurt demand for MSME products and services, resulting in continuous sharp revenue declines for many MSMEs.

There were, however, some MSMEs providing essential goods and services that benefited from increased demand as social restrictions were imposed by governments—though they were a small fraction of the surveyed MSMEs. Those reporting income increase expanded in March–April 2021 (10.9% in Indonesia, 17.0% in the Lao PDR, 15.1% in the Philippines, and 8.9% in Thailand).

3.　Impact on Employment

There were likely fewer MSMEs that cut full-time regular workers 1 year after the outbreak (Figure 3A). At the time the pandemic started in 2020, MSMEs surveyed quickly reduced the number of employees to save on operating costs (60% or more of MSMEs answered this in Indonesia, 30% or more in the Lao PDR, 37% in the Philippines, and 39% in Thailand). In March–April 2021, the share of those reducing employees in a month was a quarter or less of MSMEs surveyed (8.5% in Indonesia, 22.3% in the Lao PDR, 16.9% in the Philippines, and 26.7% in Thailand). Instead, most MSMEs reported no change in employment in the same period (90.9% in Indonesia, 63.8% in the Lao PDR, 78.8% in the Philippines, and 70.1% in Thailand).

MSMEs with temporary staffing cut decreased sharply between March–April 2020 and March–April 2021 (51.0% to 9.3% of MSMEs in Indonesia, 53.5% to 33.0% in the Lao PDR, 66.2% to 13.8% in the Philippines, and 42.3% to 22.2% in Thailand) (Figure 3B). Work-from-home (teleworking) was not feasible for MSMEs at the start of the pandemic. But 1 year later, work-from-home arrangements gradually spread among MSMEs (13.0% to 27.3% in Indonesia, 14.4% to 23.4% in the Lao PDR, 12.9% to 27.6% in the Philippines, and 21.0% to 35.5% in Thailand). This was possible due to the relatively high internet penetration of MSMEs surveyed. Around one-fifth of surveyed MSMEs continued to adjust employees' working hours in the Lao PDR (19.1%), the Philippines (18.2%), and Thailand (21.1%) in March–April 2021, except in Indonesia (9.8%). Those granting worker leaves grew in 2021 (10.8% in Indonesia, 46.8% in the Lao PDR, 20.7% in the Philippines, and 41.5% in Thailand). There was also the shift in sample groups to those with relatively good employment management a year into the pandemic.

At the time the pandemic began in 2020, a large portion of MSMEs suspended wage payments (55.8% in Indonesia, 40.6% in the Lao PDR, 56.7% in the Philippines, and 30.4% in Thailand) (Figure 4). One year later, there were around 20% or less MSMEs holding back wages (20.7% in Indonesia, 16.0% in the Lao PDR, 11.4% in the Philippines, and 12.7% in Thailand). Instead, those reporting no change in wage payment status increased (51.4% in Indonesia, 53.2% in the Lao PDR, 65.8% in the Philippines, and 58.7% in Thailand).

The share of MSMEs cutting over 30% of wage payments also fell gradually. But large wage payment cuts (over 30%) remained as the second- or the third-largest share as of March–April 2021 (14.7% in Indonesia, 10.6% in the Lao PDR, 10.4% in the Philippines, and 15.0% in Thailand).

Figure 3: Employment by MSMEs, 2020–2021

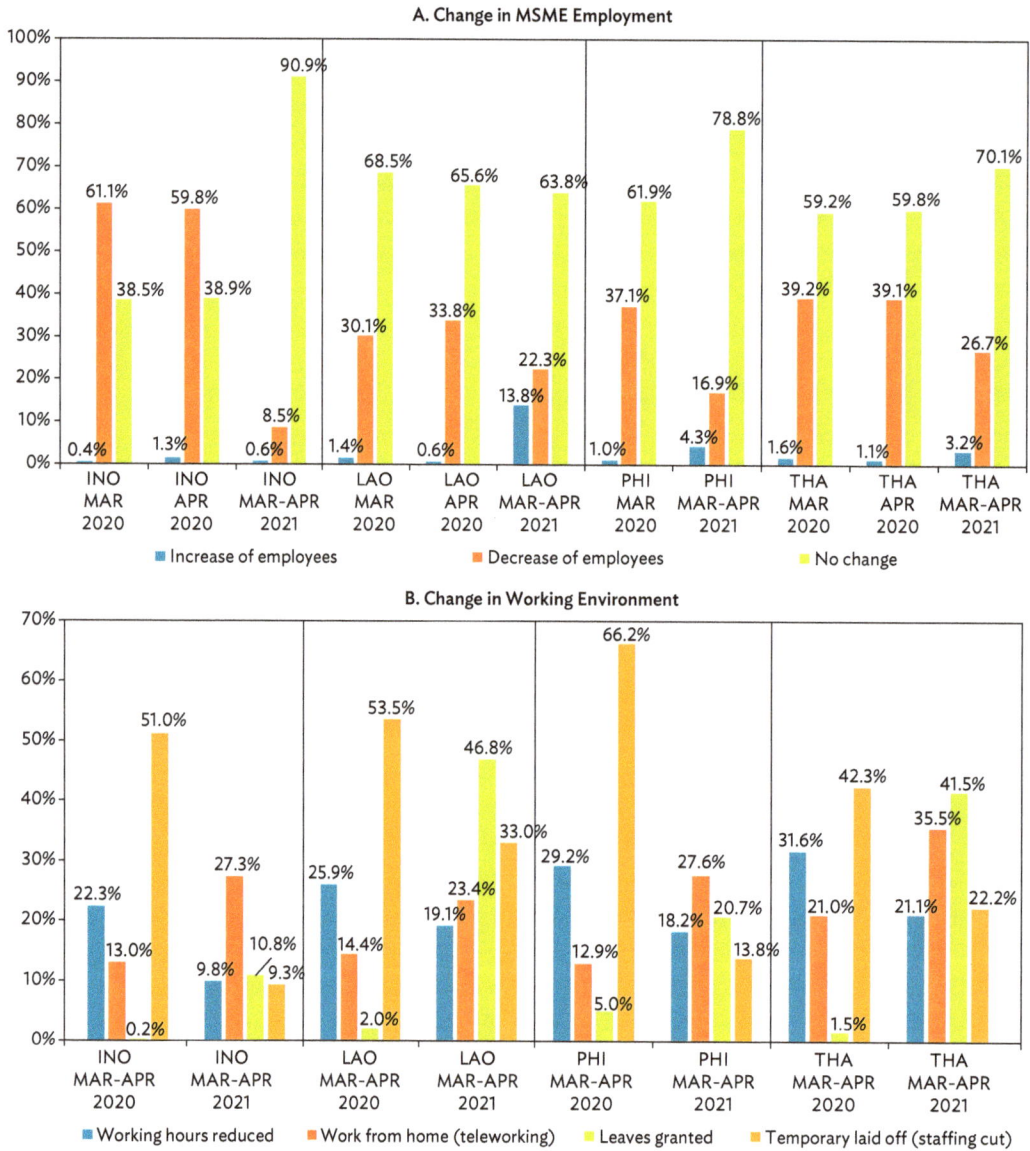

A. Change in MSME Employment

- Increase of employees
- Decrease of employees
- No change

B. Change in Working Environment

- Working hours reduced
- Work from home (teleworking)
- Leaves granted
- Temporary laid off (staffing cut)

INO = Indonesia; LAO = Lao People's Democratic Republic (Lao PDR); MSME = micro, small, and medium-sized enterprise; PHI = Philippines; THA = Thailand.

Note: For INO, 525 valid samples in March–April 2020 and 2,509 in March–April 2021; For LAO, 355 valid samples in March–April 2020 and 94 in March–April 2021; For PHI, 1,804 valid samples in March–April 2020 and 1,546 in March–April 2021; For THA, 1,147 valid samples in March–April 2020 and 963 in March–April 2021.

Source: Calculated based on MSME surveys in Indonesia, the Lao PDR, the Philippines, and Thailand, March–April 2020–2021.

Figure 4: MSME Total Wage Payments, 2020–2021

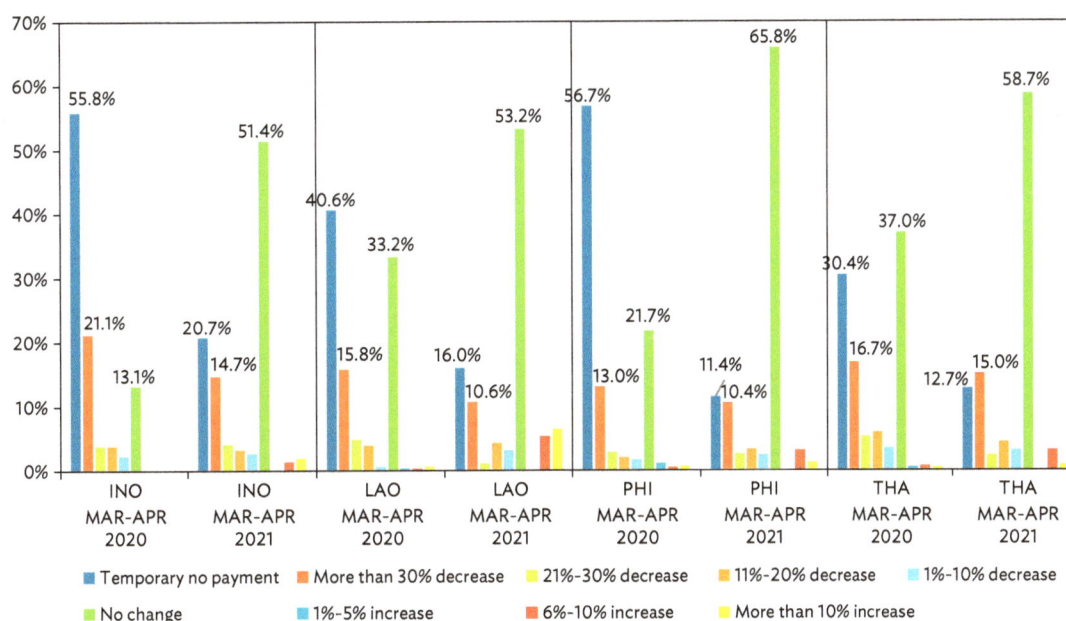

INO = Indonesia; LAO = Lao People's Democratic Republic (Lao PDR); MSME = micro, small, and medium-sized enterprise; PHI = Philippines; THA = Thailand.

Note: For INO, 525 valid samples in March–April 2020 and 2,509 in March–April 2021; For LAO, 355 valid samples in March–April 2020 and 94 in March–April 2021; For PHI, 1,804 valid samples in March–April 2020 and 1,546 in March–April 2021; For THA, 1,147 valid samples in March–April 2020 and 963 in March–April 2021.

Source: Calculated based on MSME surveys in Indonesia, the Lao PDR, the Philippines, and Thailand, March–April 2020–2021.

4.   Financial Conditions

MSMEs had to deal with a serious lack of funds at the start of the pandemic; it became a major barrier to keeping their businesses operating. Some 35%–52% of MSMEs surveyed said they had no cash or savings in March–April 2020 (52.4% in Indonesia, 35.5% in the Lao PDR, 36.7% in the Philippines, and 35.4% in Thailand) (Figure 5). Around 20%–42% of MSMEs reported funds would run out in 1 month (32.8% in Indonesia, 19.7% in the Lao PDR, 42.1% in the Philippines, and 39.8% in Thailand).

This improved 1 year after the outbreak. MSMEs with no cash and savings fell in March–April 2021 (26.1% in Indonesia, 17.0% in the Lao PDR, 23.7% in the Philippines, and 32.3% in Thailand), but they still had the top share in Thailand and the second-largest share in Indonesia and the Philippines. The share of those expected to run out of funds in 3 months was highest in Indonesia (29.3% in March–April 2021) with the second largest in Thailand (27.2%) and the Lao PDR (19.1%). Working capital shortages remained an issue for many MSMEs.

Into 2021, by contrast, MSMEs that reported holding short-term cash or savings to maintain their business grew (from 8.6% in March–April 2020 to 24.0% in March–April 2021 in Indonesia, from 37.2% to 38.3% in the Lao PDR, and from 17.0% to 35.3% in the Philippines). The exception was Thailand (19.8% to 17.1%). Again, the shift of firm groups between 2020 and 2021 may have had an effect. The most affected MSMEs in 2020 might have gone out of business, with those more successfully managing funds surviving and increasing their share in the March–April 2021 survey.

Figure 5: MSME Financial Condition, 2020–2021

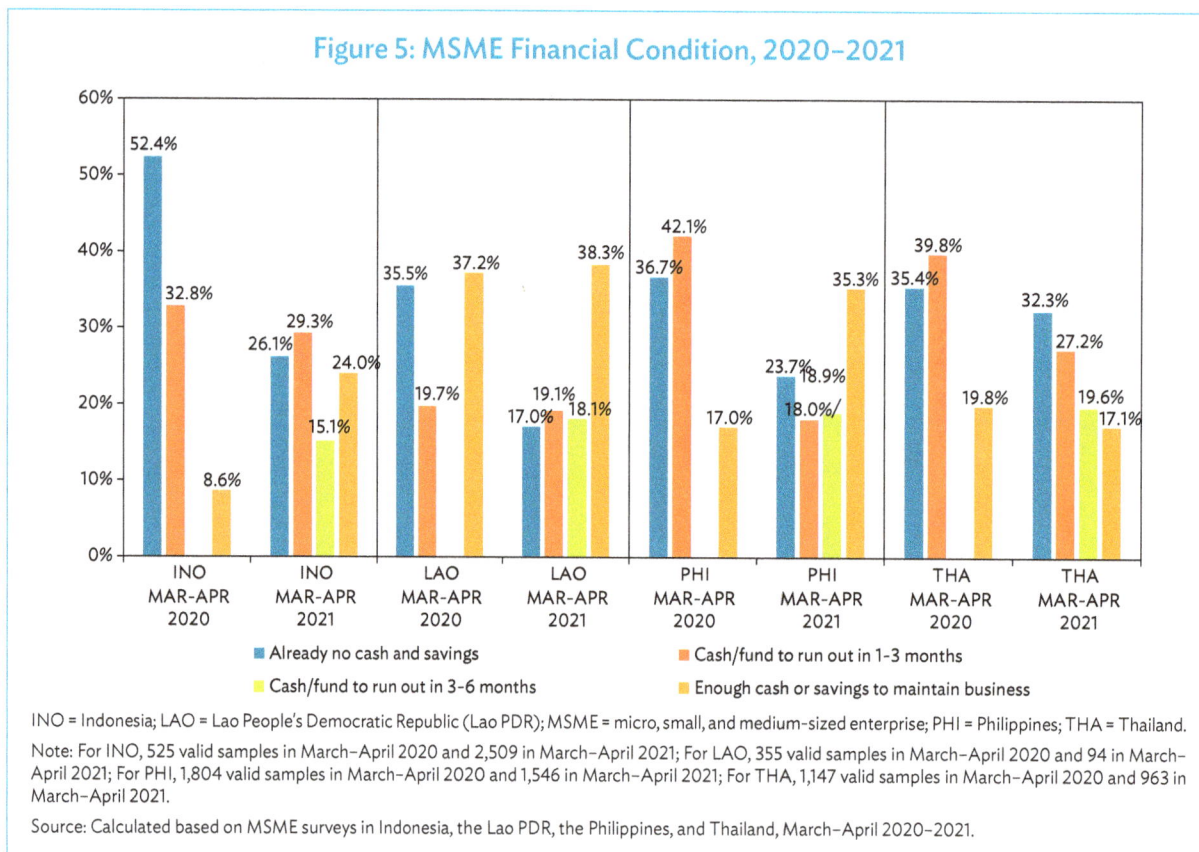

INO = Indonesia; LAO = Lao People's Democratic Republic (Lao PDR); MSME = micro, small, and medium-sized enterprise; PHI = Philippines; THA = Thailand.

Note: For INO, 525 valid samples in March–April 2020 and 2,509 in March–April 2021; For LAO, 355 valid samples in March–April 2020 and 94 in March–April 2021; For PHI, 1,804 valid samples in March–April 2020 and 1,546 in March–April 2021; For THA, 1,147 valid samples in March–April 2020 and 963 in March–April 2021.

Source: Calculated based on MSME surveys in Indonesia, the Lao PDR, the Philippines, and Thailand, March–April 2020–2021.

Traditionally, MSMEs mostly rely on their own funds and borrowing from family, relatives, and friends to operate their businesses. This did not change during the pandemic. Those using their own funds to maintain operations had the largest share in March–April 2021 (68.8% in Indonesia, 28.7% in the Lao PDR, 35.1% in the Philippines, and 36.9% in Thailand) (Figure 6). Those borrowing from close relatives and friends accounted for 22.6% of surveyed MSMEs in Indonesia, 22.3% in the Lao PDR, 21.5% in the Philippines, and 34.3% in Thailand; holding the second largest share.

Although dependence on informal financing remained high, it has gradually been reduced. Instead, access to bank credit gradually expanded. MSMEs borrowing from banks increased from an average of 5% in March–April 2020 to 17% in March–April 2021 (from 1.0% to 12.2% in Indonesia, from 7.6% to 21.3% in the Lao PDR, from 4.8% to 10.0% in the Philippines, and from 7.5% to 24.6% in Thailand). Coupled with those applying for bank loans, the share with access to bank credit grew from an average of 22% in March–April 2020 to 39% in March–April 2021 (from 9.7% to 21.0% in Indonesia, from 23.9% to 61.7% in the Lao PDR, from 21.5% to 18.0% in the Philippines, and from 32.8% to 54.3% in Thailand). Large amounts of government financial assistance through refinancing facilities, subsidized loans, and credit guarantees helped. Accordingly, MSME demand for government funding support increased (from 2.3% in March–April 2020 to 9.7% in March–April 2021 in Indonesia, from 0.3% to 6.4% in the Lao PDR, from 5.7% to 6.9% in the Philippines, and from 2.0% to 2.8% in Thailand).

A year into the pandemic, digital finance platforms such as peer-to-peer lending and crowdfunding were not a funding option among most MSMEs, except in the Lao PDR (0.5% in Indonesia, 10.6% in the Lao PDR, 1.7% in the Philippines, and 2.0% in Thailand during March–April 2021).

Figure 6: MSME Funding, 2020–2021

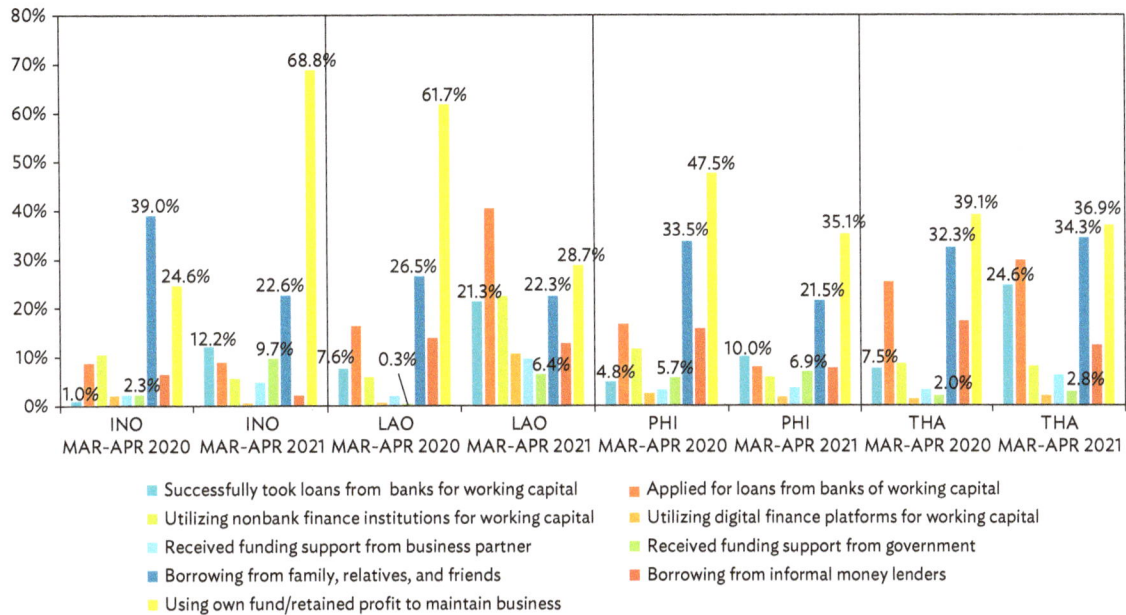

INO = Indonesia; LAO = Lao People's Democratic Republic (Lao PDR); MSME = micro, small, and medium-sized enterprise; PHI = Philippines; THA = Thailand.

Note: For INO, 525 valid samples in March–April 2020 and 2,509 in March–April 2021; For LAO, 355 valid samples in March–April 2020 and 94 in March–April 2021; For PHI, 1,804 valid samples in March–April 2020 and 1,546 in March–April 2021; For THA, 1,147 valid samples in March–April 2020 and 963 in March–April 2021.

Source: Calculated based on MSME surveys in Indonesia, the Lao PDR, the Philippines, and Thailand, March–April 2020–2021.

Thematic Impact

This section breaks down the analysis to specific groups: (i) tourism-related MSMEs; (ii) digitally operated MSMEs; (iii) internationalized MSMEs; and (iv) women-led MSMEs. Government mobility restrictions—including travel bans—severely damaged tourism. The pandemic accelerated the ongoing digitalization of businesses. Supply chain disruptions and a drop in foreign demand brought about by national mobility restrictions hit globalized MSMEs hardest. And women-led MSMEs—a critical MSME segment—needed to continue innovating to contribute to economic growth. What was the pandemic's impact on all these during the first year?

1.   Tourism-Related MSMEs

In the August–September 2020 and March–April 2021 surveys, tourism-related firms were defined as those who declared being a member of tourism organizations or associations. They included restaurants, hotels, tour services, transportation services, and souvenir shops. Figure 7 shows a gap in the survey response ratio between tourism-related MSMEs and non-tourism MSMEs. The blue bar indicates a higher impact (a higher percentage share) in tourism-related firms, with the red one showing the opposite. The upper bar is for August–September 2020 and the lower for March–April 2021.[9]

Tourism-related MSMEs accounted for less than 20% of surveyed MSMEs (Table 3). Overall, the business environment for the tourism sector remained dismal during the first year of the pandemic, affected by the prolonged pandemic and frequently adopted national mobility restrictions. In Indonesia, the drop in foreign demand (from tourists), delayed delivery of products and services, created supply chain disruptions and contract cancellations affected tourism MSMEs more than non-tourism MSMEs (Figure 7A). In the Philippines, a drop in both domestic and foreign demand, supply chain disruptions, and contract cancellations dramatically reduced tourism-related MSMEs during the year, resulting in higher temporary closures than non-tourism MSMEs (Figure 7B). Thailand followed a similar trend; higher foreign demand loss, supply disruptions, contract cancellations, and temporary business closures in tourism-related MSMEs throughout a year (Figure 7C).

---

[9]   Tourism-related firms can also be extracted from the March–April 2020 survey, but the way tourism was categorized differed from the second and third surveys. Thus, this subsection compares the August–September 2020 and March–April 2021 surveys. The Lao PDR was excluded from this analysis due to a lack of survey data.

Figure 7: Business Environment—Tourism-Related MSMEs, 2020–2021

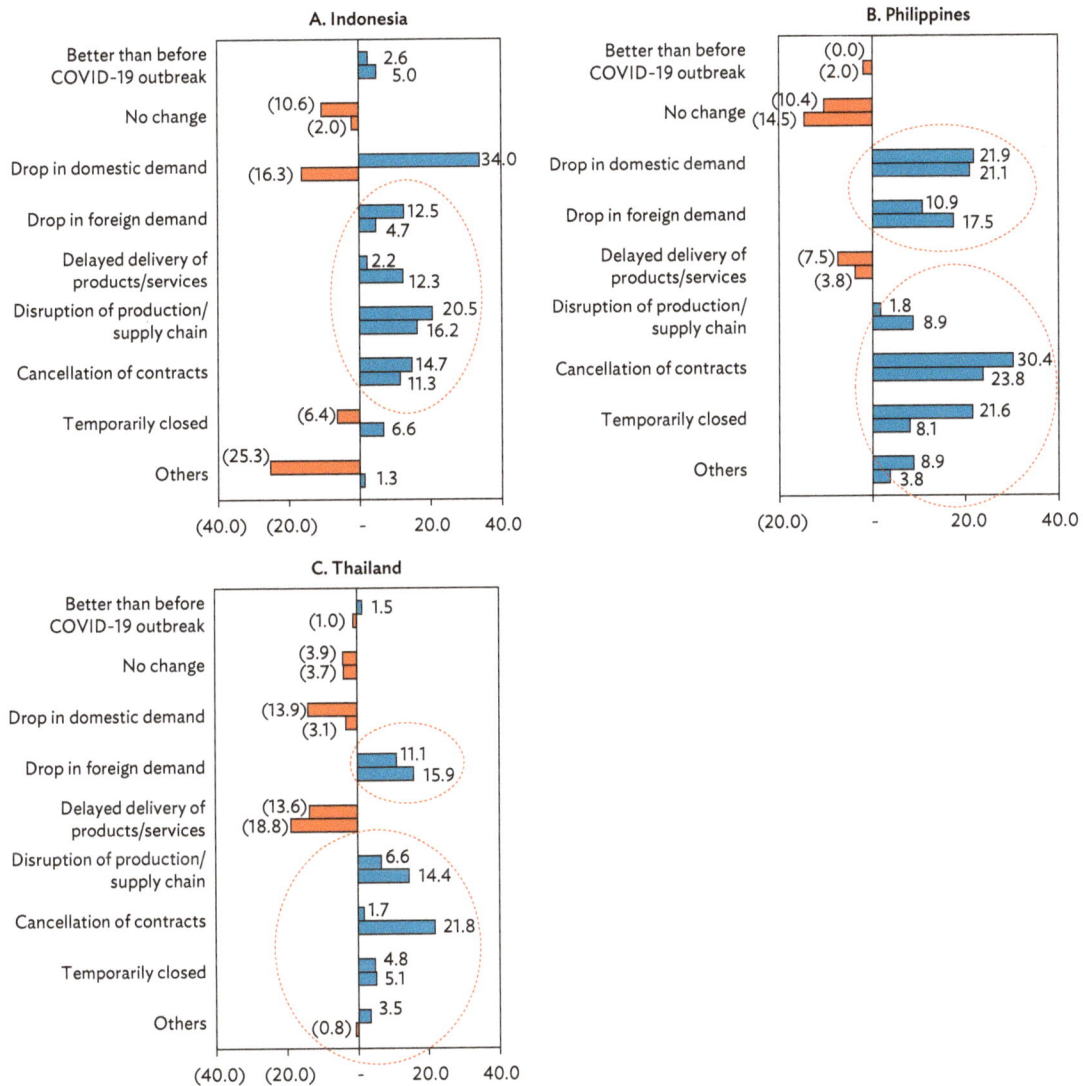

COVID-19 = coronavirus disease; MSME = micro, small, and medium-sized enterprise.

Notes: The upper band is for August–September 2020 with the lower band for March–April 2021. The gap in percentage shares of tourism-related MSMEs (firms who are members of tourism organizations/associations) and non-tourism MSMEs. Blue bars are the percentage points (survey response ratio) higher in tourism-related MSMEs than non-tourism MSMEs. Red bars reflect the opposite. For Indonesia, there were 128 valid samples in August–September 2020 and 2,509 in March–April 2021; For the Philippines, 686 valid samples in August–September 2020 and 1,546 in March–April 2021; For Thailand, 520 valid samples in August–September 2020 and 963 in March–April 2021.

Source: Calculated based on MSME surveys in Indonesia, the Philippines, and Thailand, August–September 2020 and March–April 2021.

In short, tourism-related MSMEs remained stymied a year after the outbreak. In the tourism sector, zero-revenue or temporarily closed MSMEs and/or MSMEs with over 30% revenue losses were more likely to appear and worsen 1 year into the pandemic (Figure 8). Indonesia promoted tourism as part of its stimulus packages from the start of the pandemic in 2020, especially for major tourist destinations like Bali. The Philippines and Thailand also allocated national budgets to stimulate tourism spending in 2020. Despite these assistance programs, tourism-related MSMEs had not recovered as of March–April 2021.

Figure 8: Revenue—Tourism-Related MSMEs, 2020–2021

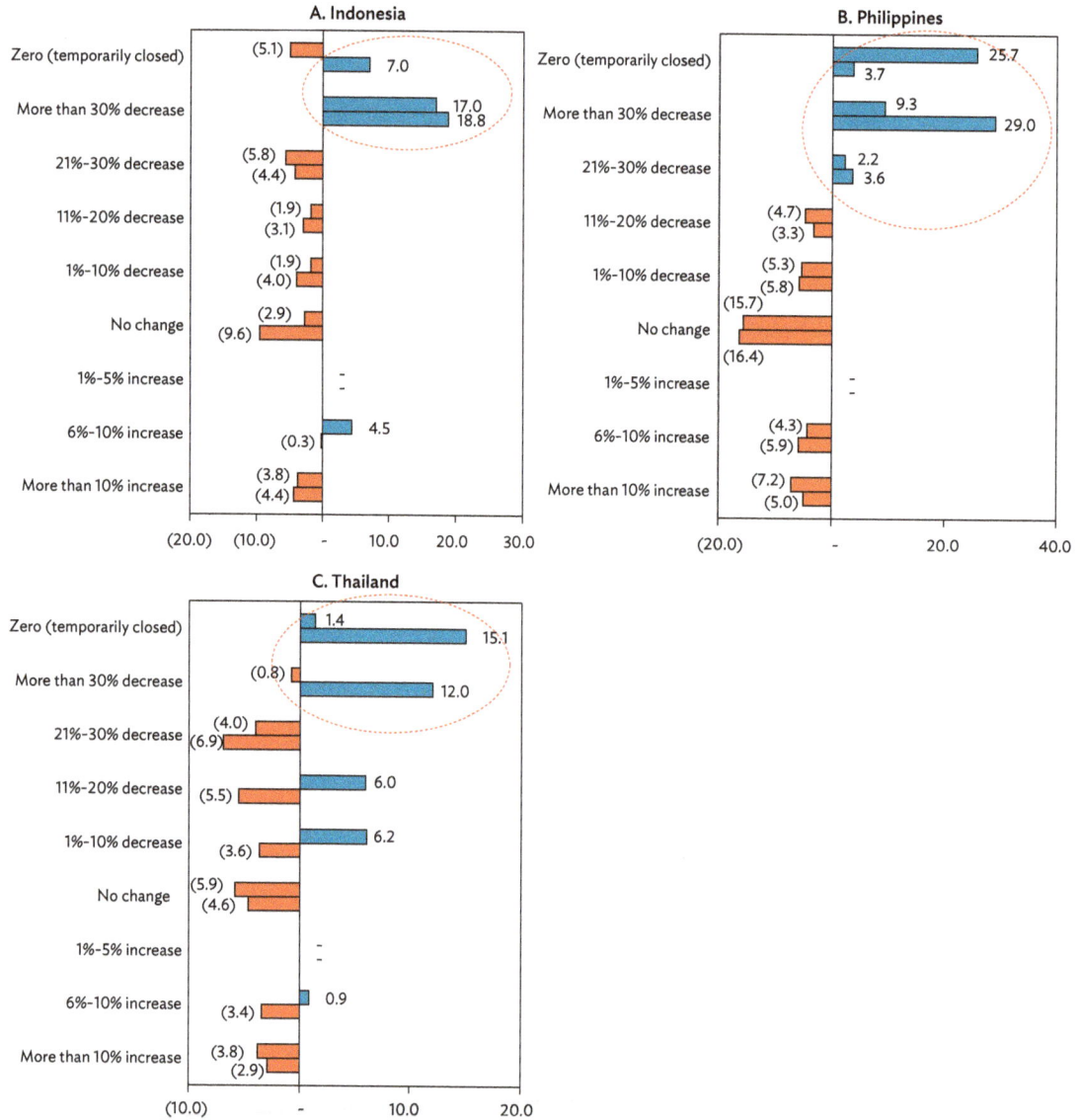

A. Indonesia

Category	Value (upper)	Value (lower)
Zero (temporarily closed)	(5.1)	7.0
More than 30% decrease	17.0	18.8
21%–30% decrease	(5.8)	(4.4)
11%–20% decrease	(1.9)	(3.1)
1%–10% decrease	(1.9)	(4.0)
No change	(2.9)	(9.6)
1%–5% increase	–	–
6%–10% increase	4.5	(0.3)
More than 10% increase	(3.8)	(4.4)

B. Philippines

Category	Value (upper)	Value (lower)
Zero (temporarily closed)	25.7	3.7
More than 30% decrease	9.3	29.0
21%–30% decrease	2.2	3.6
11%–20% decrease	(4.7)	(3.3)
1%–10% decrease	(5.3)	(5.8)
No change	(15.7)	(16.4)
1%–5% increase	–	–
6%–10% increase	(4.3)	(5.9)
More than 10% increase	(7.2)	(5.0)

C. Thailand

Category	Value (upper)	Value (lower)
Zero (temporarily closed)	1.4	15.1
More than 30% decrease	(0.8)	12.0
21%–30% decrease	(4.0)	(6.9)
11%–20% decrease	6.0	(5.5)
1%–10% decrease	6.2	(3.6)
No change	(5.9)	(4.6)
1%–5% increase	–	–
6%–10% increase	0.9	(3.4)
More than 10% increase	(3.8)	(2.9)

MSME = micro, small, and medium-sized enterprise.

Notes: The upper band is for August–September 2020 with the lower band for March–April 2021. The gap in percentage shares of tourism-related MSMEs (firms who are members of tourism organizations/associations) and non-tourism MSMEs. Blue bars are the percentage points (survey response ratio) higher in tourism-related MSMEs than non-tourism MSMEs. Red bars reflect the opposite. For Indonesia, there were 128 valid samples in August–September 2020 and 2,509 in March–April 2021; For the Philippines, 686 valid samples in August–September 2020 and 1,546 in March–April 2021; For Thailand, 520 valid samples in August–September 2020 and 963 in March–April 2021.

Source: Calculated based on MSME surveys in Indonesia, the Philippines, and Thailand, August–September 2020 and March–April 2021.

2.   Digitally Operated MSMEs

Here we compare the pandemic impact between August–September 2020 and March–April 2021, with digitally operated firms defined as those who are engaged in selling goods and services online or e-commerce.[10] The pandemic and mobility restrictions were an incentive for more MSMEs to go digital. But digitally operated MSMEs were not always successful given the pandemic. The impact of the drop in demand, supply disruptions, and contract cancellations were likely higher in digitally operated MSMEs than non-digital firms surveyed, while those who reported better a business environment than prior to COVID-19 increased in digitally operated MSMEs, although they were a small fraction (Figure 9).

Figure 9: Business Environment—Digitally Operated MSMEs, 2020–2021

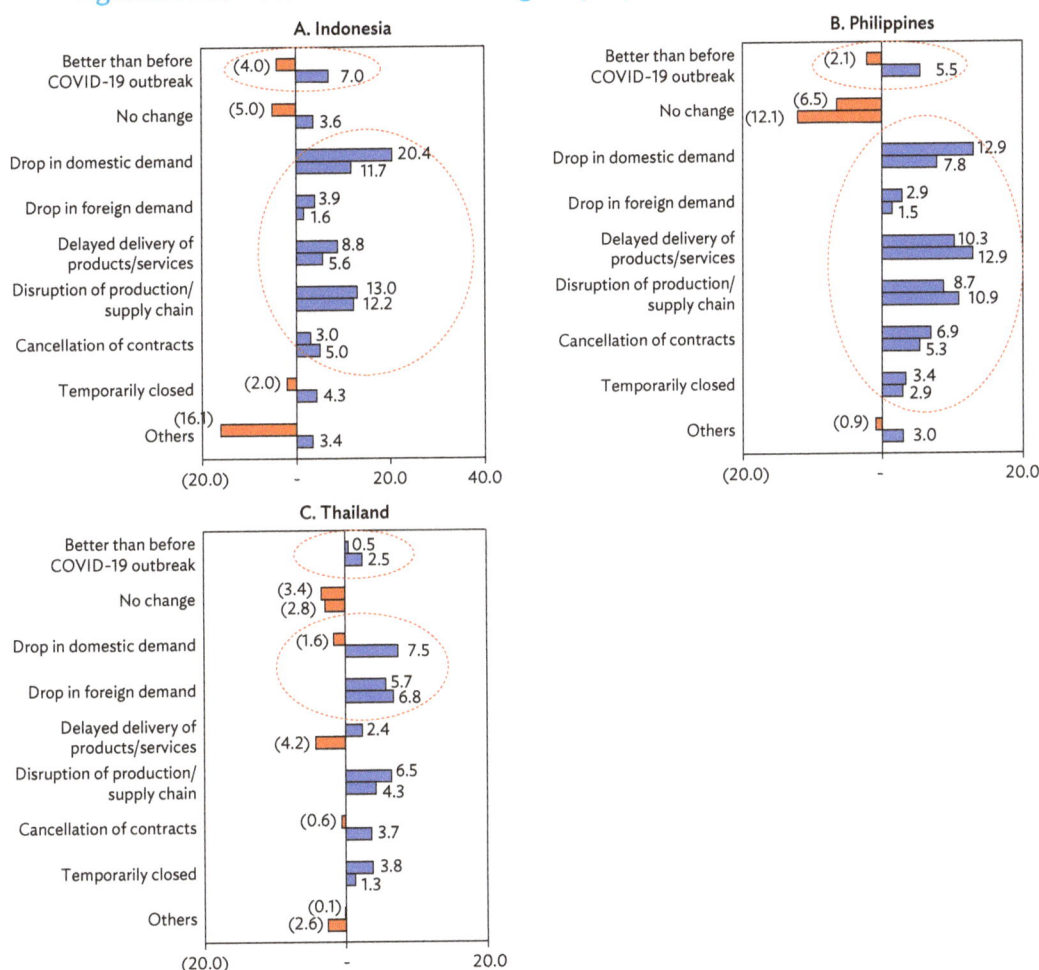

COVID-19 = coronavirus disease; MSME = micro, small, and medium-sized enterprise.

Notes: The upper band is for August–September 2020 with the lower band for March–April 2021. The gap in percentage shares of digitally operated MSMEs (firms engaged in online selling or e-commerce) and non-digital MSMEs. Blue bars are the percentage points (survey response ratio) higher in digitally operated MSMEs than non-digital MSMEs. Red bars reflect the opposite. For Indonesia, there were 128 valid samples in August–September 2020 and 2,509 in March–April 2021; For the Philippines, 686 valid samples in August–September 2020 and 1,546 in March–April 2021; For Thailand, 520 valid samples in August–September 2020 and 963 in March–April 2021.

Source: Calculated based on MSME surveys in Indonesia, the Philippines, and Thailand, August–September 2020 and March–April 2021.

---

[10]   Digitally operated firms can be also extracted from the March–April 2020 survey, but the way they were categorized differed from the second and third surveys. Thus, this section compares the August–September 2020 and March–April 2021 surveys. The Lao PDR was excluded from this analysis due to a lack of survey data.

The profitability of digitally operated MSMEs was mixed during the pandemic. In Indonesia, the share of those with a more than 6% income increase was likely higher in digitally operated MSMEs than non-digital MSMEs in August–September 2020 (Figure 10A). They were mainly small firms selling essential daily goods, food, and health-care products and delivering them. However, toward 2021, the share of those with no revenue or more than a 30% decrease in income likely increased in digitally operated MSMEs than non-digital MSMEs. They were mainly firms involved with nonessential goods and services. In the Philippines, those profitable and less profitable co-existed among digitally operated MSMEs, with two streams of businesses—those which were hurt by the pandemic and those which benefited. This became clearer toward 2021 (Figure 10B). Thailand followed a similar trend as Indonesia (Figure 10C).

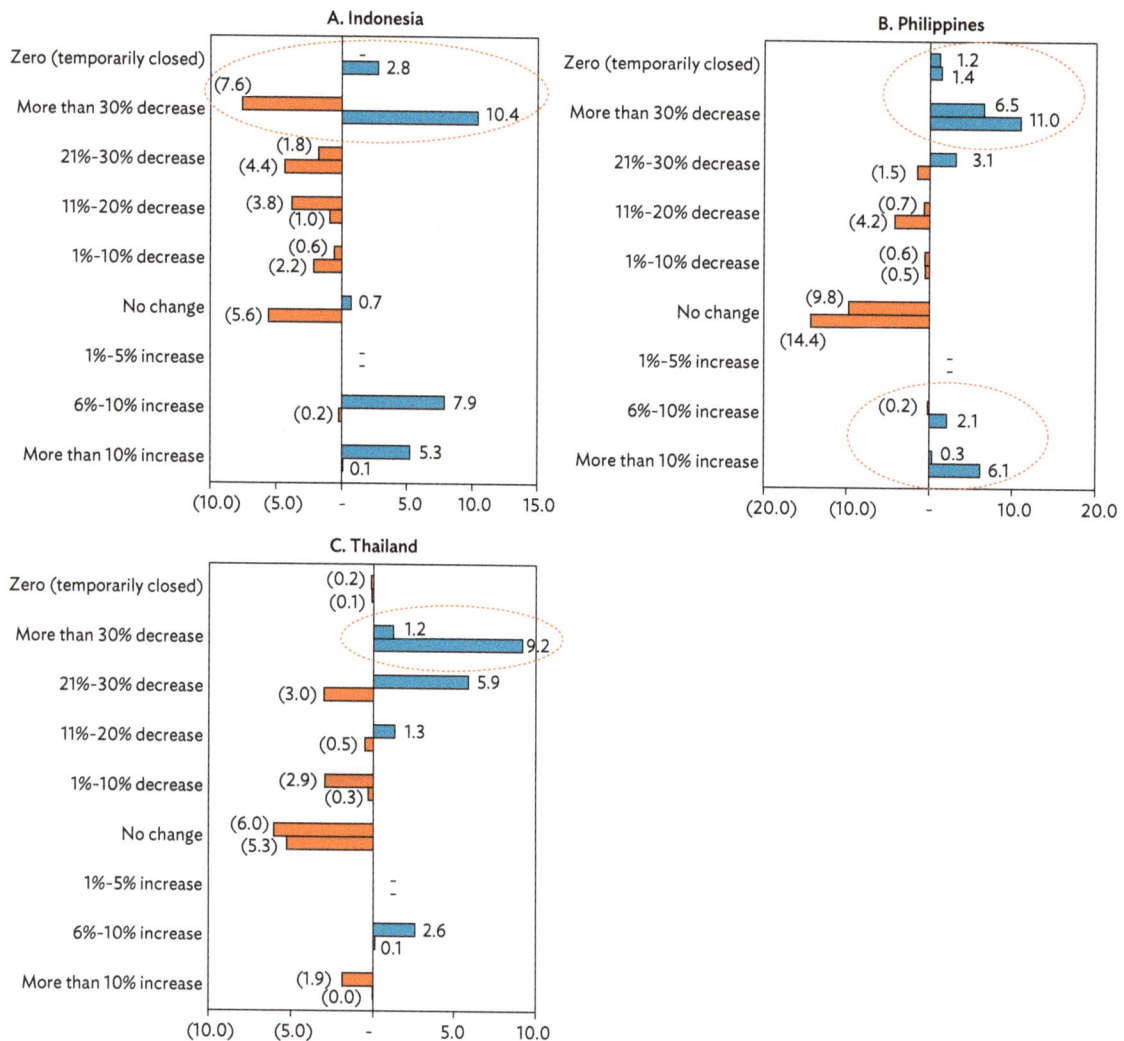

Figure 10: Revenue—Digitally Operated MSMEs, 2020–2021

MSME = micro, small, and medium-sized enterprise.

Notes: The upper band is for August–September 2020 with the lower band for March–April 2021. The gap in percentage shares of digitally operated MSMEs (firms engaged in online selling or e-commerce) and non-digital MSMEs. Blue bars are the percentage points (survey response ratio) higher in digitally operated MSMEs than non-digital MSMEs. Red bars reflect the opposite. For Indonesia, there were 128 valid samples in August–September 2020 and 2,509 in March–April 2021; For the Philippines, 686 valid samples in August–September 2020 and 1,546 in March–April 2021; For Thailand, 520 valid samples in August–September 2020 and 963 in March–April 2021.

Source: Calculated based on MSME surveys in Indonesia, the Philippines, and Thailand, August–September 2020 and March–April 2021.

This suggests MSMEs that retained demand—such as essential goods and services, daily products, and food—could continue to operate successfully. As the pandemic wore on, other MSMEs dealing with nonessential products and services likely faced greater operational difficulties, even if digitalized (e-commerce).

3.   Women-Led MSMEs

The pandemic had a mixed impact on women-led MSMEs—or MSMEs run or owned by a woman. Some faced a sharp drop in demand, supply disruptions, and saw their business hurt more by the pandemic harder than men-led MSMEs. Others reported a better business environment than before the pandemic (except in Indonesia) (Figure 11). This subsection compares the impact on women-led MSMEs between March–April 2020 and March–April 2021. Similar to the previous subsections, the blue bar indicates a higher impact (a higher percentage share) in women-led MSMEs compared with men-led MSMEs, and the red band shows the opposite.

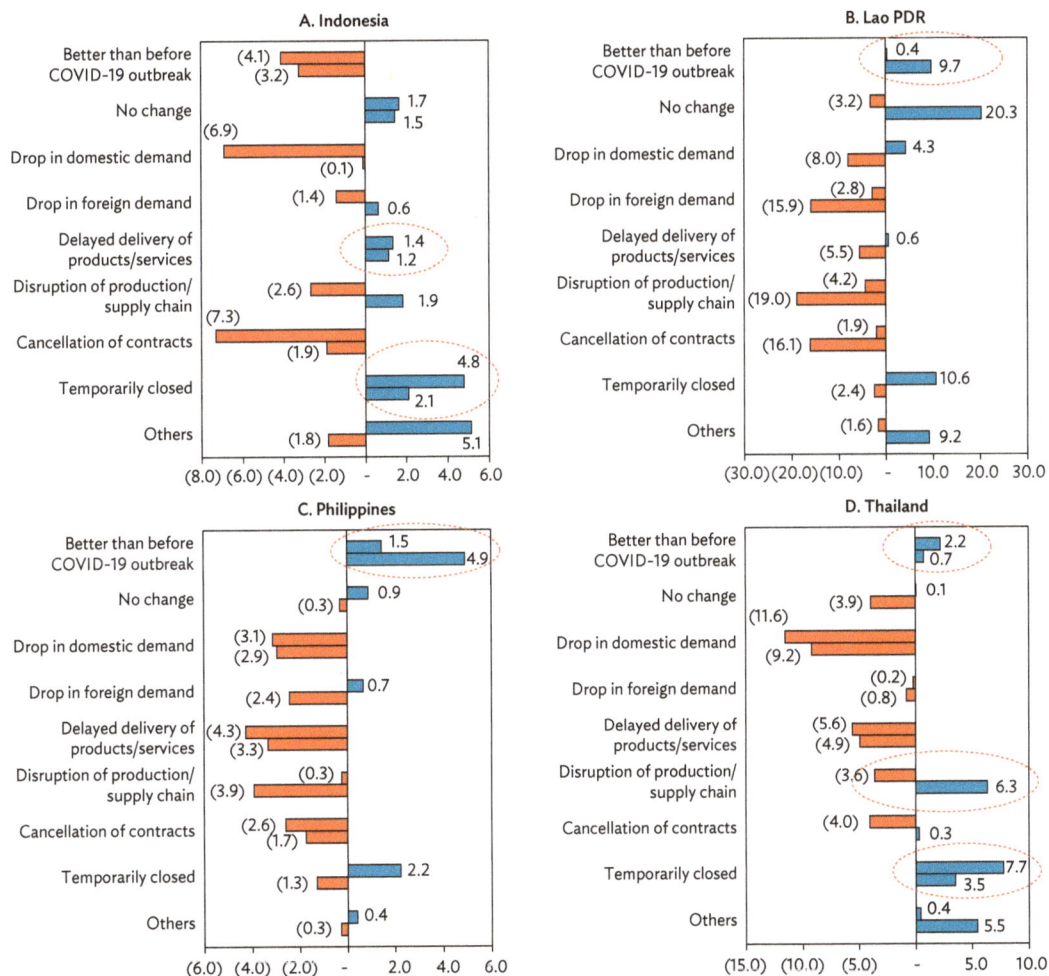

Figure 11: Business Environment—Women-Led MSMEs, 2020–2021

COVID-19 = coronavirus disease; LAO = Lao People's Democratic Republic (Lao PDR); MSME = micro, small, and medium-sized enterprise.

Notes: The upper band is for March–April 2020 with the lower band for March–April 2021. The gap in percentage shares of women-led MSMEs (firms owned/managed by women) and men-led MSMEs. Blue bars are the percentage points (survey response ratio) higher in women-led MSMEs than men-led MSMEs. Red bars reflect the opposite. For Indonesia, there were 525 valid samples in March–April 2020 and 2,509 in March–April 2021; For the Lao People's Democratic Republic (Lao PDR), 355 valid samples in March–April 2020 and 94 in March–April 2021; For the Philippines, 1,804 valid samples in March–April 2020 and 1,546 in March–April 2021; For Thailand, 1,147 valid samples in March–April 2020 and 963 in March–April 2021.

Source: Calculated based on MSME surveys in Indonesia, the Lao PDR, the Philippines, and Thailand, March–April 2020–2021.

In Indonesia, the business environment for women-led MSMEs was harsh throughout the first year of the pandemic (Figure 11A). While the share of those reporting no change was slightly higher than men-led MSMEs, women-led MSMEs were more likely to face supply disruptions, delayed product delivery, and temporary business closures than men-led MSMEs. In the Lao PDR, women-led MSMEs more likely improved their business conditions than men-led MSMEs into 2021, where those reporting a better business environment likely increased (Figure 11B). The Philippines followed the same trend as the Lao PDR (Figure 11C). In Thailand, women-led MSMEs were similar to Indonesia, but the share of those reporting a better business environment was just slightly higher than men-led MSMEs (Figure 11D).

Revenues for women-led MSMEs varied by country, but roughly split into two groups: those with no revenue or a sharp decrease (Indonesia and Thailand) and those seeing high profits even during the pandemic (the Lao PDR and the Philippines) (Figure 12). Women-led MSMEs with higher revenues were more likely in digital operations than men-led MSMEs (see Box).

Figure 12: Revenue—Women-Led MSMEs, 2020–2021

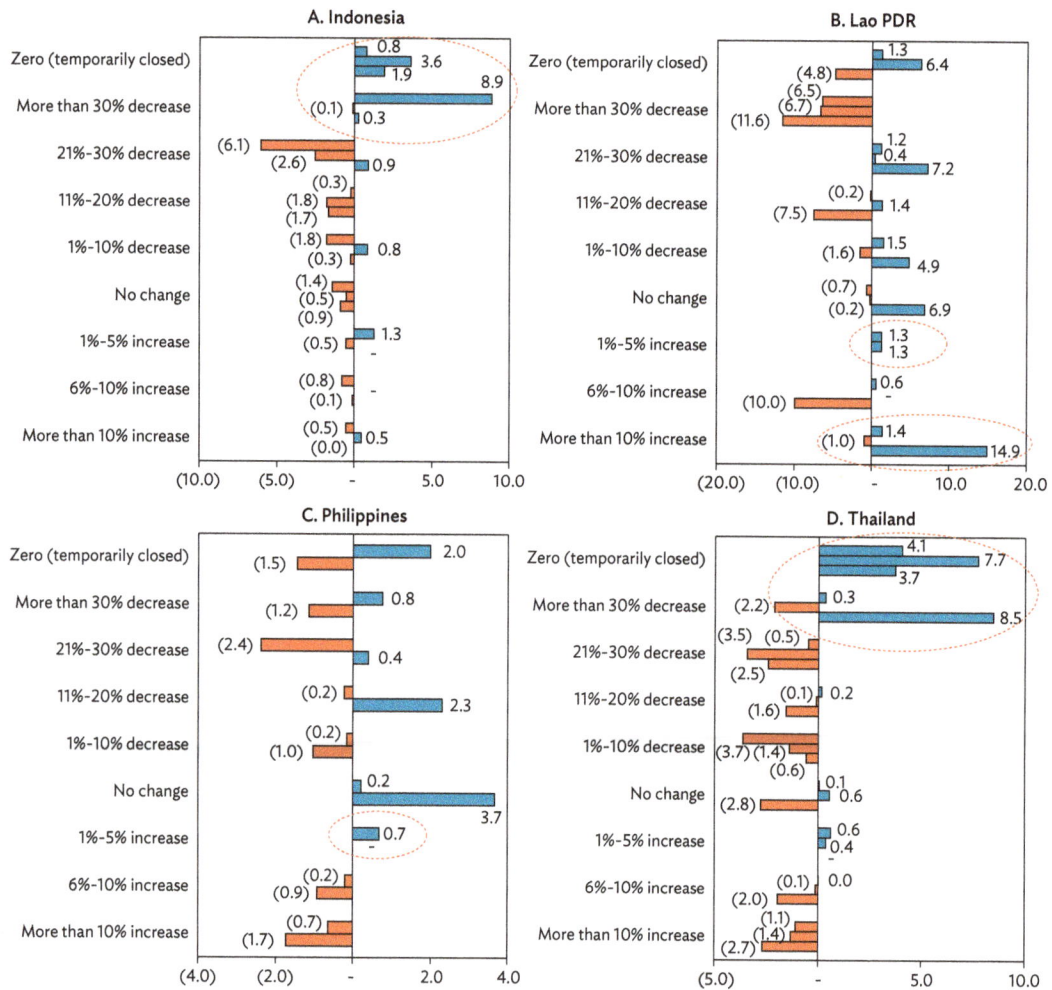

LAO = Lao People's Democratic Republic (Lao PDR); MSME = micro, small, and medium-sized enterprise.

Notes: The upper band is for March 2020, the middle band is for April 2020, and the lower band is for March–April 2021. There is no middle bar for the Philippines. The gap in percentage shares of women-led MSMEs (firms owned/managed by female) and men-led MSMEs. Blue bars are the percentage points (survey response ratio) higher in women-led MSMEs than men-led MSMEs. Red bars reflect the opposite. For Indonesia, there were 525 valid samples in March–April 2020 and 2,509 in March–April 2021; For the Lao People's Democratic Republic (Lao PDR), 355 valid samples in March–April 2020 and 94 in March–April 2021; For the Philippines, 1,804 valid samples in March–April 2020 and 1,546 in March–April 2021; For Thailand, 1,147 valid samples in March–April 2020 and 963 in March–April 2021.

Source: Calculated based on MSME surveys in Indonesia, the Lao PDR, the Philippines, and Thailand, March–April 2020–2021.

Box: Digitally Operated Women-Led MSMEs Managed Their Work Environment and Gained Relatively More Than Others During the Pandemic in Indonesia

In March–April 2021, around half of the micro, small, and medium-sized enterprises (MSMEs) surveyed were women-led MSMEs in Indonesia. They are a critical driver of the economy, and many are innovative in operations. Some 28% of MSMEs were those selling their goods and services online or engaged in e-commerce, with most women-led.

As with others, the pandemic hit digitally operated women-led MSMEs hardest. But the magnitude of the impact was relatively lower than non-digital women-led MSMEs (Figure B.1). Both digital and non-digital women-led MSMEs improved operations into 2021. But the level of decreased domestic demand was likely lower in the digital firms surveyed. Digitally operated men-led MSMEs faced a similar impact as digitally operated women-led MSMEs; in general, digitally operated firms were able to manage operations during the pandemic regardless of gender ownership.

In terms of income, digitally operated women-led MSMEs did relatively better than others (Figure B.2). The share of those reporting more than a 10% increase in income were more likely in digitally operated women-led MSMEs than non-digital women-led MSMEs and digital/non-digital men-led MSMEs in 2021—although the difference was trivial among surveyed MSMEs.

Digitally operated women-led MSMEs were basically able to manage their work environment, increasing working-style options—such as work-from-home (teleworking) and granted employee leaves—-and reducing layoffs during the first year of the pandemic (Figure B.3). This likely helped adjust operational and managerial costs, allowing higher profits to digitally operated women-led MSMEs amid the pandemic.

Figure B.1: MSME Business Environment in Indonesia, 2020–2021

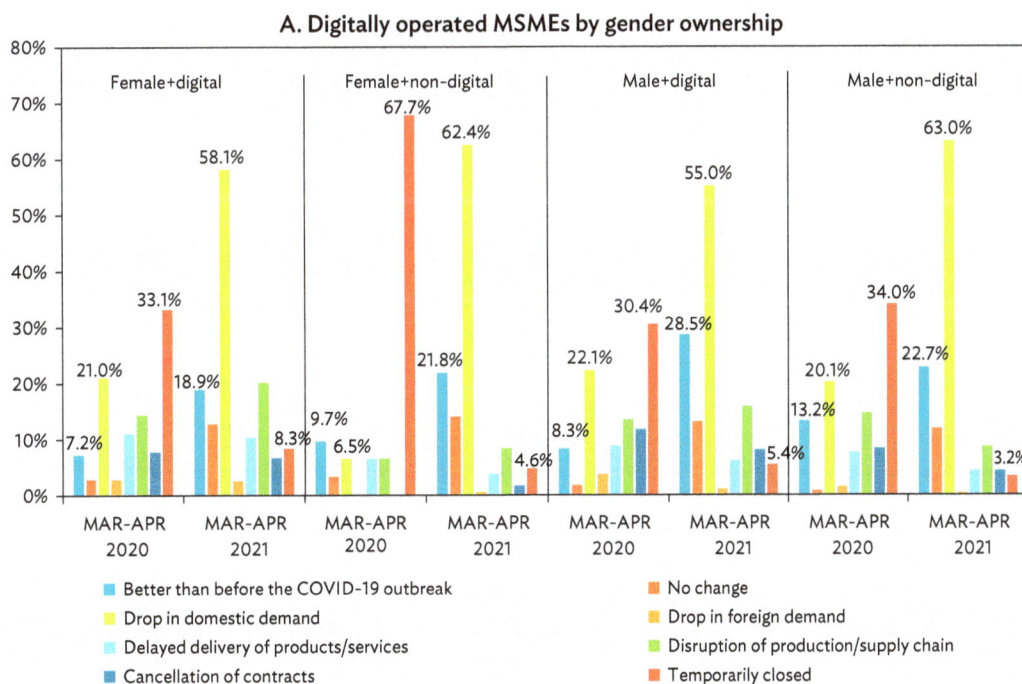

A. Digitally operated MSMEs by gender ownership

continued on next page

Box   *continued*

B. Gap between March–April 2020 and March–April 2021

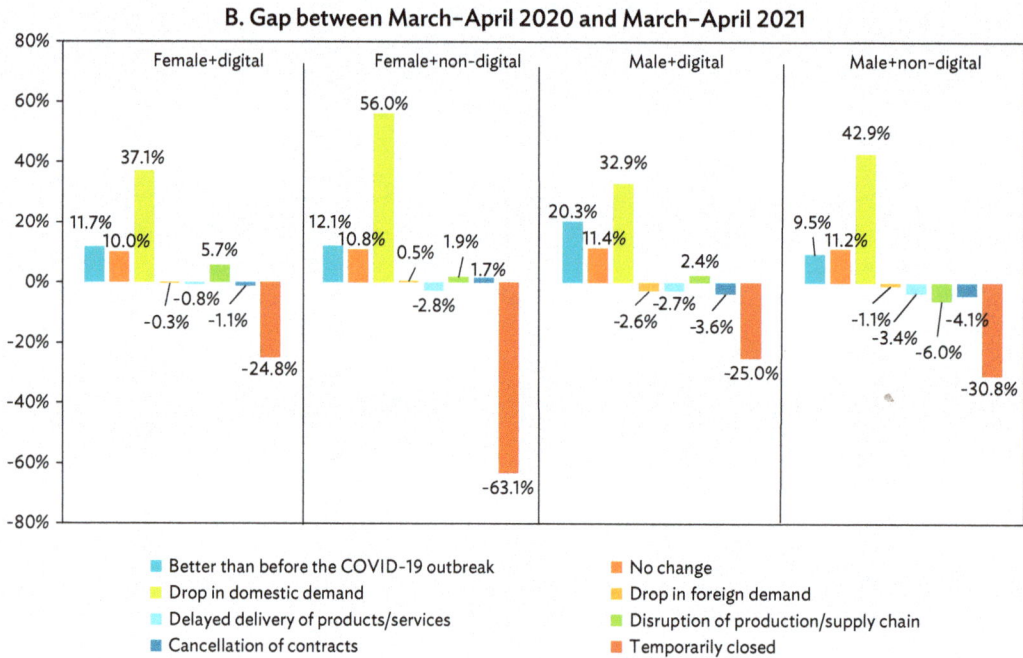

Legend:
- Better than before the COVID-19 outbreak
- Drop in domestic demand
- Delayed delivery of products/services
- Cancellation of contracts
- No change
- Drop in foreign demand
- Disruption of production/supply chain
- Temporarily closed

COVID-19 = coronavirus disease; MSME = micro, small, and medium-sized enterprise.

Note: Valid samples from the MSME Surveys in Indonesia: 525 (March–April 2020), 119 of which were digitally operated women-led MSMEs (Female+digital); 37 were women-led MSMEs with no e-commerce/internet use (Female+non-digital); 256 were digitally operated men-led MSMEs (Male+digital); 113 were men-led-MSMEs with no e-commerce and internet use (Male+non-digital). There were 2,509 valid samples in March–April 2021: 408 were female+digital; 841 female+non-digital; 298 male+digital, and 962 male+non-digital. A digitally operated MSME is defined as a firm selling goods and services online (e-commerce) and/or with internet use for business. For Figure B, the gap is calculated as the share of categorized MSMEs in March–April 2021 minus that in March–April 2020.

Figure B.2: MSME Monthly Income in Indonesia, 2020–2021

A. Digitally operated MSMEs by gender ownership

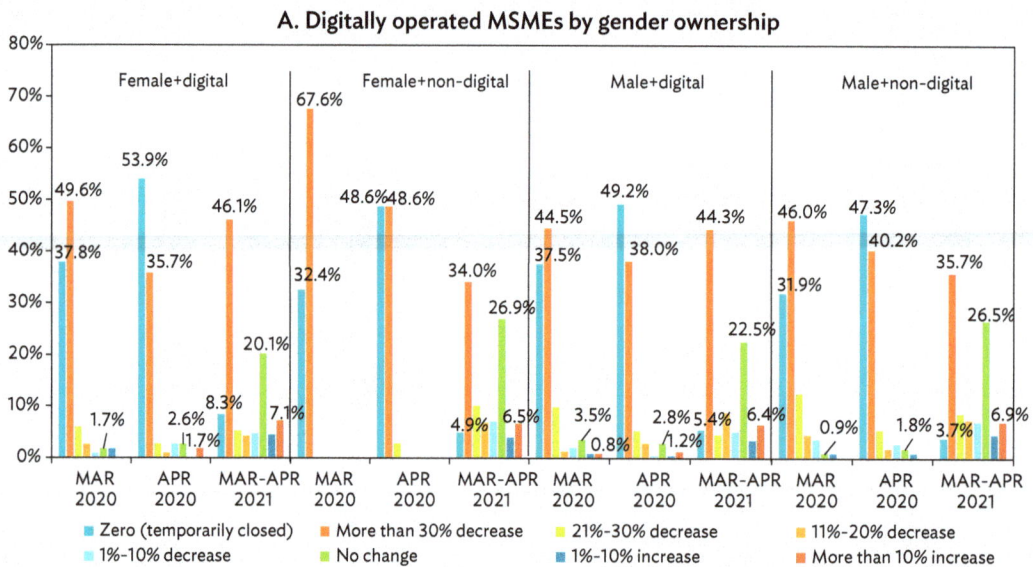

Legend:
- Zero (temporarily closed)
- More than 30% decrease
- 21%–30% decrease
- 11%–20% decrease
- 1%–10% decrease
- No change
- 1%–10% increase
- More than 10% increase

continued on next page

Box   *continued*

B. Gap between March 2020 and March–April 2021

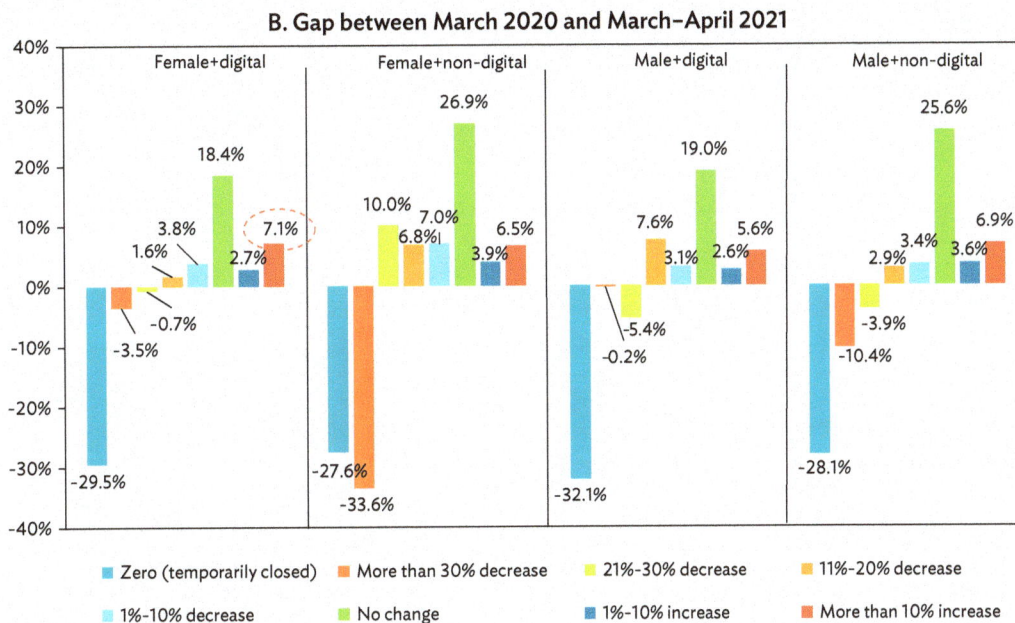

Female+digital
- -29.5%
- -3.5%
- 1.6%
- -0.7%
- 3.8%
- 18.4%
- 2.7%
- 7.1%

Female+non-digital
- -27.6%
- -33.6%
- 10.0%
- 6.8%
- 7.0%
- 26.9%
- 3.9%
- 6.5%

Male+digital
- -32.1%
- -0.2%
- -5.4%
- 7.6%
- 3.1%
- 19.0%
- 2.6%
- 5.6%

Male+non-digital
- -28.1%
- -10.4%
- -3.9%
- 2.9%
- 3.4%
- 25.6%
- 3.6%
- 6.9%

Legend:
- ■ Zero (temporarily closed)
- ■ More than 30% decrease
- ■ 21%–30% decrease
- ■ 11%–20% decrease
- ■ 1%–10% decrease
- ■ No change
- ■ 1%–10% increase
- ■ More than 10% increase

MSME = micro, small, and medium-sized enterprise.

Note: Valid samples from the MSME Surveys in Indonesia: 525 (March–April 2020), 119 of which were digitally operated women-led MSMEs (Female+digital); 37 were women-led MSMEs with no e-commerce/internet use (Female+non-digital); 256 were digitally operated men-led MSMEs (Male+digital); 113 were men-led-MSMEs with no e-commerce and internet use (Male+non-digital). There were 2,509 valid samples in March–April 2021: 408 were female+digital; 841 female+non-digital; 298 male+digital, and 962 male+non-digital. A digitally operated MSME is defined as a firm selling goods and services online (e-commerce) and/or with internet use for business. For Figure B, the gap is calculated as the share of categorized MSMEs in March–April 2021 minus that in March 2020.

Figure B.3: Change in MSME Working Environment in Indonesia, 2020–2021

A. Digitally operated MSMEs by gender ownership

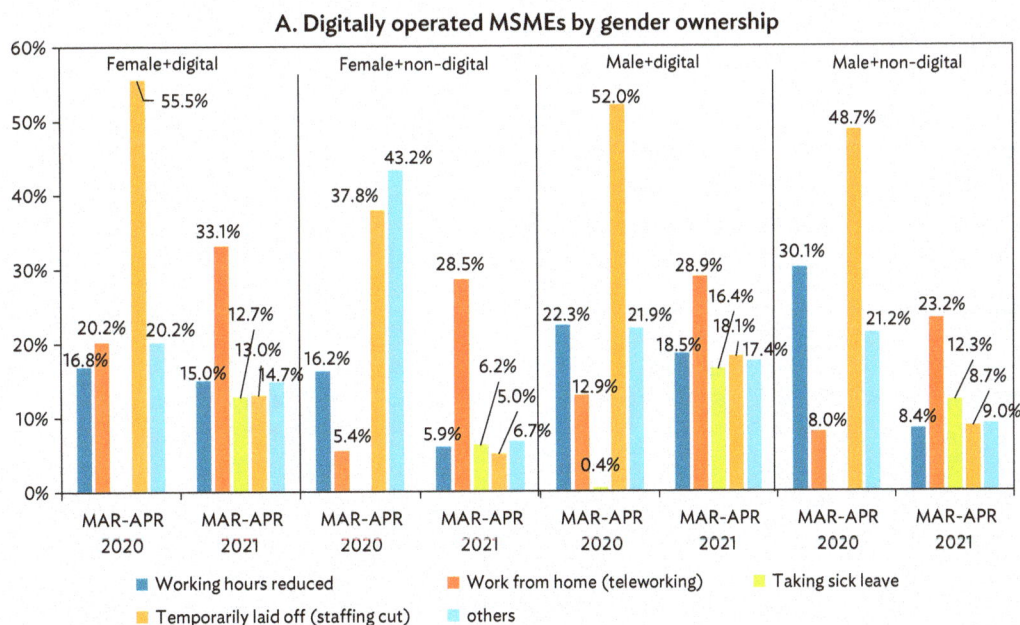

Legend:
- ■ Working hours reduced
- ■ Work from home (teleworking)
- ■ Taking sick leave
- ■ Temporarily laid off (staffing cut)
- ■ others

continued on next page

Box   *continued*

B. Gap between March–April 2020 and March–April 2021

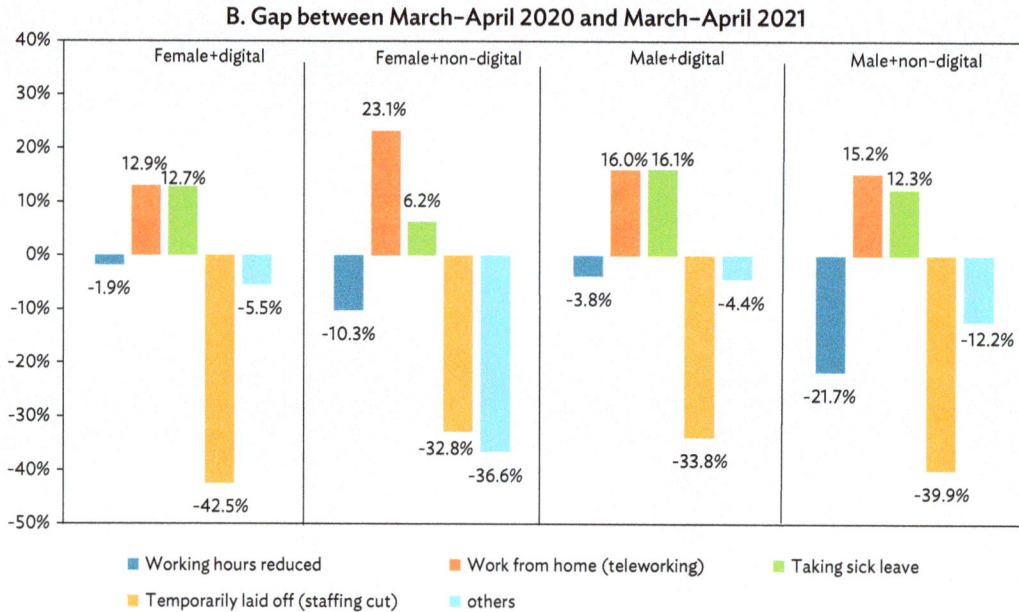

MSME = micro, small, and medium-sized enterprise.

Note: Valid samples from the MSME Surveys in Indonesia: 525 (March–April 2020), 119 of which were digitally operated women-led MSMEs (Female+digital); 37 were women-led MSMEs with no e-commerce/internet use (Female+non-digital); 256 were digitally operated men-led MSMEs (Male+digital); 113 were men-led-MSMEs with no e-commerce and internet use (Male+non-digital). There were 2,509 valid samples in March–April 2021: 408 were female+digital; 841 female+non-digital; 298 male+digital, and 962 male+non-digital. A digitally operated MSME is defined as a firm selling goods and services online (e-commerce) and/or with internet use for business. For Figure B, the gap is calculated as the share of categorized MSMEs in March–April 2021 minus that in March–April 2020.

Source: Calculated based on MSME surveys in Indonesia, the Lao PDR, the Philippines, and Thailand, March–April 2020–2021.

4.   Internationalized MSMEs

Lockdowns and social restrictions limited the business of internationalized MSMEs during the first year of the pandemic. In ADB surveys, internationalized MSMEs are defined as those involved in global supply chains or export/import business. Here we compare the impact on internationalized MSMEs between March–April 2020 and March–April 2021. The blue bar indicates a higher impact (a higher percentage share) in internationalized MSMEs compared with domestically focused MSMEs, and the red band shows the opposite.

One year into the pandemic, foreign demand continued to drop. There were continued delays in product deliveries along with supply chain disruptions and high contract cancellations, more so for internationalized MSMEs than domestically focused MSMEs (Figure 13). The series of national lockdowns and frequent mobility restrictions hurt the international operations of MSMEs. In Indonesia and the Lao PDR, those reporting a better business environment appeared in 2021, but they were a small fraction of internationalized MSMEs. The countries surveyed had begun economic recovery as consumption and exports rose. But the survey results suggest the benefits of improved exports had yet to reach MSME exporters.

Meanwhile, the share of those reporting temporary business closures was lower in internationalized MSMEs than domestically focused MSMEs, except in Indonesia. This suggests internationalized MSMEs in the Lao PDR, the Philippines, and Thailand were more likely to continue operations using accumulated cash and savings to cover pandemic losses.

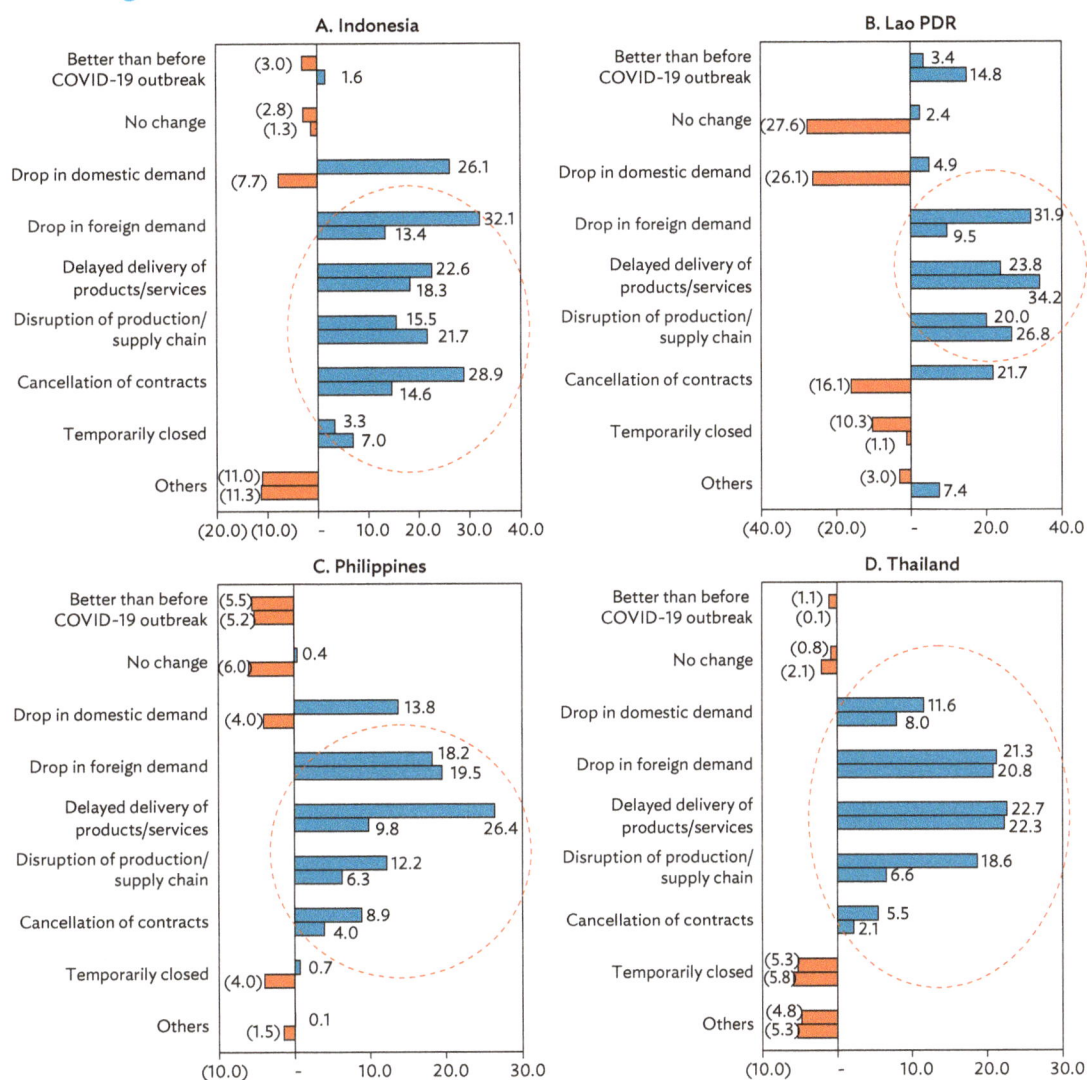

Figure 13: Business Environment—Internationalized MSMEs, 2020–2021

A. Indonesia

Category	2020	2021
Better than before COVID-19 outbreak	(3.0)	1.6
No change	(2.8)	(1.3)
Drop in domestic demand	26.1	(7.7)
Drop in foreign demand	32.1	13.4
Delayed delivery of products/services	22.6	18.3
Disruption of production/supply chain	15.5	21.7
Cancellation of contracts	28.9	14.6
Temporarily closed	3.3	7.0
Others	(11.0)	(11.3)

B. Lao PDR

Category	2020	2021
Better than before COVID-19 outbreak	3.4	14.8
No change	(27.6)	2.4
Drop in domestic demand	(26.1)	4.9
Drop in foreign demand	31.9	9.5
Delayed delivery of products/services	23.8	34.2
Disruption of production/supply chain	20.0	26.8
Cancellation of contracts	(16.1)	21.7
Temporarily closed	(10.3)	(1.1)
Others	(3.0)	7.4

C. Philippines

Category	2020	2021
Better than before COVID-19 outbreak	(5.5)	(5.2)
No change	(6.0)	0.4
Drop in domestic demand	13.8	(4.0)
Drop in foreign demand	18.2	19.5
Delayed delivery of products/services	9.8	26.4
Disruption of production/supply chain	12.2	6.3
Cancellation of contracts	8.9	4.0
Temporarily closed	0.7	(4.0)
Others	0.1	(1.5)

D. Thailand

Category	2020	2021
Better than before COVID-19 outbreak	(1.1)	(0.1)
No change	(0.8)	(2.1)
Drop in domestic demand	11.6	8.0
Drop in foreign demand	21.3	20.8
Delayed delivery of products/services	22.7	22.3
Disruption of production/supply chain	18.6	6.6
Cancellation of contracts	5.5	2.1
Temporarily closed	(5.3)	(5.8)
Others	(4.8)	(5.3)

COVID-19 = coronavirus disease; LAO = Lao People's Democratic Republic (Lao PDR); MSME = micro, small, and medium-sized enterprise.

Notes: The upper band is for March–April 2020 with the lower band for March–April 2021. The gap in percentage shares of internationalized MSMEs (firms involved in the global supply chain or export/import business) and domestic-focused MSMEs. Blue bars are the percentage points (survey response ratio) higher in internationalized MSMEs than domestic-focused MSMEs. Red bars reflect the opposite. For Indonesia, there were 525 valid samples in March–April 2020 and 2,509 in March–April 2021; For the Lao PDR, 355 valid samples in March–April 2020 and 94 in March–April 2021; For the Philippines, 1,804 valid samples in March–April 2020 and 1,546 in March–April 2021; For Thailand, 1,147 valid samples in March–April 2020 and 963 in March–April 2021.

Source: Calculated based on MSME surveys in Indonesia, the Lao PDR, the Philippines, and Thailand, March–April 2020–2021.

Many of the internationalized MSMEs surveyed lost large amounts of income, while some firms increased revenues. In Indonesia, the share of those reporting no revenue remained higher in internationalized MSMEs a year into the pandemic, while those with increased income (more than 10%) likely grew into 2021 (Figure 14A). In the Lao PDR, those with a sharp declining incomes (more than 30%) increased somewhat in internationalized MSMEs, while there were also those with higher incomes (more than 10%) (Figure 14B). The Philippines followed a similar trend as in the Lao PDR (Figure 14C). Thailand was similar to the Lao PDR and the Philippines, but the co-existence of profitable and less profitable internationalized MSMEs was more evident than domestically focused firms into 2021 (Figure 14D). The pandemic likely created two clusters of businesses among internationalized MSMEs—those devastated by the pandemic and social restrictions and those which better managed the shocks. These included digitally operated MSMEs.

Figure 14: Revenue—Internationalized MSMEs, 2020–2021

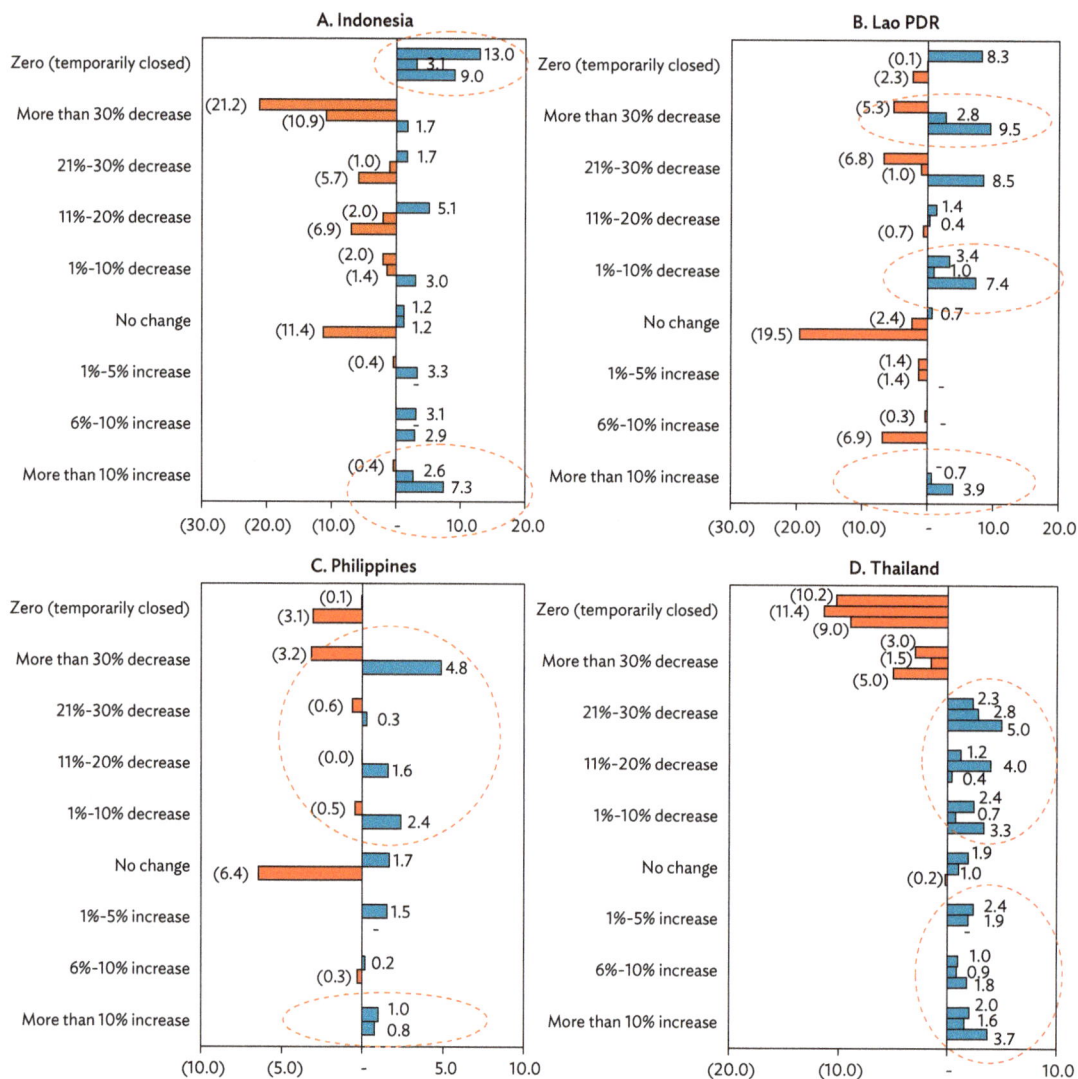

LAO = Lao People's Democratic Republic (Lao PDR); MSME = micro, small, and medium-sized enterprise.

Notes: The upper band is for March 2020, the middle band is for April 2020, and the lower band is for March–April 2021. There is no middle bar for the Philippines. The gap in percentage shares of internationalized MSMEs (firms involved in the global supply chain or export/import business) and domestic-focused MSMEs. Blue bars are the percentage points (survey response ratio) higher in internationalized MSMEs than domestic-focused MSMEs. Red bars reflect the opposite. For Indonesia, there were 525 valid samples in March–April 2020 and 2,509 in March–April 2021; For the Lao PDR, 355 valid samples in March–April 2020 and 94 in March–April 2021; For the Philippines, 1,804 valid samples in March–April 2020 and 1,546 in March–April 2021; For Thailand, 1,147 valid samples in March–April 2020 and 963 in March–April 2021.

Source: Calculated based on MSME surveys in Indonesia, the Lao PDR, the Philippines, and Thailand, March–April 2020–2021.

Policy Implications

The prolonged pandemic increases downside risks for national economic growth. The possibility of new coronavirus variant outbreaks and the return of mobility restrictions increase business uncertainty. What strategies should MSME owners and managers apply to maintain their business? What government assistance do they want to survive the pandemic and recovery? How can governments respond to the demand from MSMEs and help them grow further during and after the pandemic?

1.   MSME Perceptions of the COVID-19 Impact

The ADB surveys monitored what actions MSMEs would take if the pandemic continues further. Their priorities varied by country (Figure 15). In Indonesia, finance was a top concern for MSMEs in 2020. They wanted financial institutions to allow delayed repayments (46.9% of surveyed MSMEs), followed by reduced wage payments (29.9%) and applying for bankruptcy (20.8%). One year later, their needs shifted to internal cost management,

Figure 15: Actions Considered by MSMEs, 2020–2021

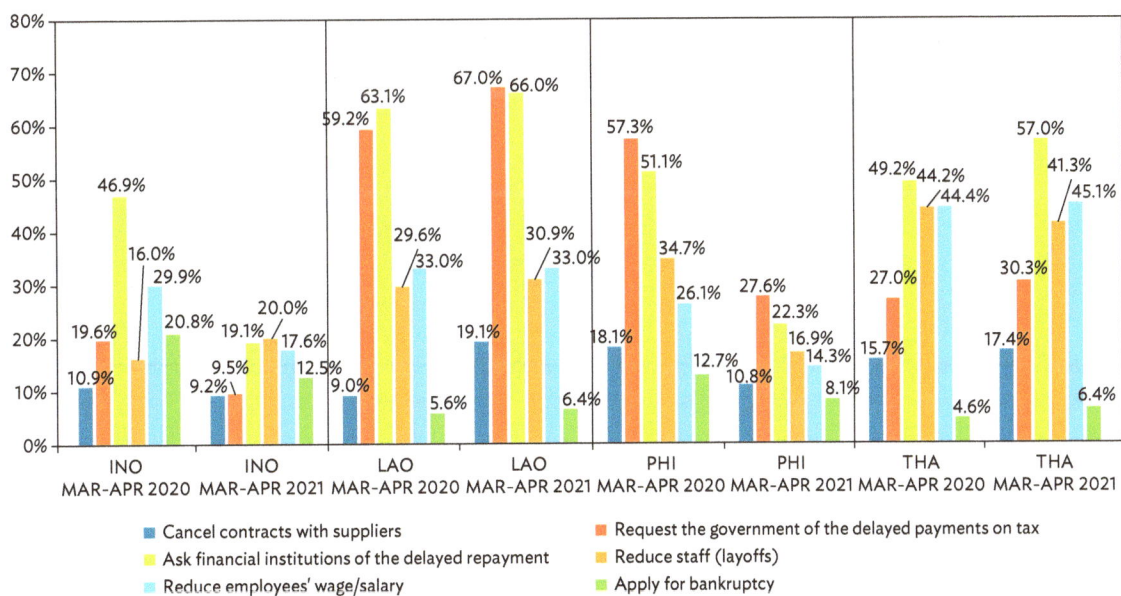

Legend:
- Cancel contracts with suppliers
- Ask financial institutions of the delayed repayment
- Reduce employees' wage/salary
- Request the government of the delayed payments on tax
- Reduce staff (layoffs)
- Apply for bankruptcy

INO = Indonesia; LAO = Lao People's Democratic Republic (Lao PDR); MSME = micro, small, and medium-sized enterprise; PHI = Philippines; THA = Thailand.

Note: For INO, 525 valid samples in March–April 2020 and 2,509 in March–April 2021; For LAO, 355 valid samples in March–April 2020 and 94 in March–April 2021; For PHI, 1,804 valid samples in March–April 2020 and 1,546 in March–April 2021; For THA, 1,147 valid samples in March–April 2020 and 963 in March–April 2021.

Source: Calculated based on MSME surveys in Indonesia, the Lao PDR, the Philippines, and Thailand, March–April 2020–2021.

where staffing cuts (layoffs) ranked first (20.0%), followed by a request for delayed loan repayments (19.1%) and reduced wage payments (17.6%). In the Lao PDR, tax payments and loan repayments were top concerns among surveyed MSMEs 1 year into the pandemic (60% or more requested delays of these payments). The Philippines followed the same trend as the Lao PDR. In Thailand, MSMEs' top concern was loan repayments (57.0% of MSMEs in March–April 2021), followed by wage payments (45.1%) and staffing cuts (41.3%).

Overall, MSMEs surveyed struggled to reduce costs to maintain business during the prolonged pandemic, including further layoffs in the future. This suggests that better cost management is needed for MSMEs to survive, given the continuing pandemic and possible outbreaks of new coronavirus variants. Continuing to accelerate digitalization of MSME operations and administration is one among several options to reduce costs. Assistance should be elaborated to promote digitalization of MSMEs for improving their cost control and marketing. For example, organized training programs and/or business development services on digitalization would benefit MSME owners and managers.

2.   Policy Measures Desired by MSMEs

While governments used a variety of social restrictions—some more strict than others—to contain the spread of COVID-19, they also provided a wide range of emergency assistance programs for households and private businesses, including MSMEs and their workers, with or without large-scale economic stimulus packages. Based on existing policy measures, the ADB surveys also asked MSME owners and managers what policy measures were most needed to support their business during the pandemic.

Figure 16 shows the MSME responses to finance-related policy measures, with answers "strongly needed" or "somewhat needed." Since the first survey was conducted in 2020, debt finance assistance was the most popularly desired government support among MSMEs. The majority of MSMEs continued to ask for concessional loans, including zero-interest loans and collateral-free loans throughout the first year of the pandemic.

More than half of MSMEs surveyed answered "strong or somewhat needed" for all items, but the top three finance policy support measures they desired slightly differed by country. In Indonesia, zero-interest/collateral-free loans ranked first in 2020 (95.6% of the surveyed MSMEs), followed by debtor-in-possession financing (90.7%) and special refinance/low-interest loans (89.7%). In 2021, the top three were all about access to credit (68.4% for zero-interest and/or collateral-free loans, 63.1% for faster loan approval, and 61.8% for refinance/low-interest loans). At the time the pandemic began in 2020, most MSMEs were pessimistic, with many considering bankruptcy. With repeating respondents over surveys just 1.2% in Indonesia, many surveyed in 2020 might have gone out of business, with those surviving into 2021 seeking more working capital financing to maintain business operations.

In the Lao PDR, the top three in 2020 were all about access to credit (90.7% for zero-interest/collateral-free loans, 87.0% for refinance/low-interest loans, and 83.9% for faster loan approval). In 2021, it was "facilitating access to new financing models or digital financial services" (79.8%), followed by zero-interest/collateral-free loans (74.5%) and debtor-in-possession financing (74.5%). Into 2021, MSMEs started considering digital finance as an alternative funding tool, but the MSME business environment was slower to recover in the Lao PDR, as many considered a financing scheme that facilitates their business closures.

In the Philippines, the top three on the wish list were all about access to credit in both 2020 and 2021 (94.6% in 2020 and 78.2% in 2021 for zero-interest/collateral-free loans, 89.6% and 76.8% for faster loan approvals, and 89.5% and 74.7% for refinanced/low-interest loans). One year into the pandemic, access to working capital financing was the most serious concern for MSMEs.

Figure 16: Financial Policy Measures Desired by MSMEs, 2020–2021

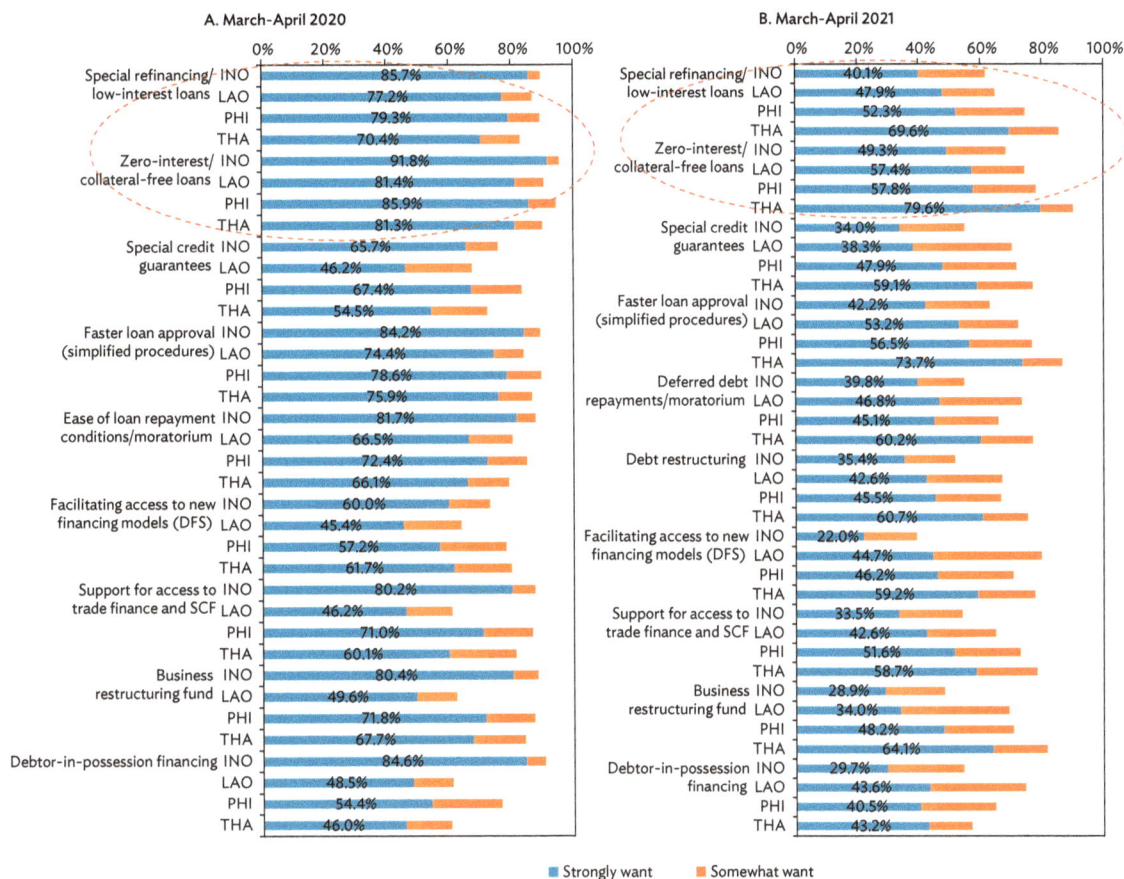

A. March-April 2020

Measure	Country	Strongly want
Special refinancing/low-interest loans	INO	85.7%
	LAO	77.2%
	PHI	79.3%
	THA	70.4%
Zero-interest/collateral-free loans	INO	91.8%
	LAO	81.4%
	PHI	85.9%
	THA	81.3%
Special credit guarantees	INO	65.7%
	LAO	46.2%
	PHI	67.4%
	THA	54.5%
Faster loan approval (simplified procedures)	INO	84.2%
	LAO	74.4%
	PHI	78.6%
	THA	75.9%
Ease of loan repayment conditions/moratorium	INO	81.7%
	LAO	66.5%
	PHI	72.4%
	THA	66.1%
Facilitating access to new financing models (DFS)	INO	60.0%
	LAO	45.4%
	PHI	57.2%
	THA	61.7%
Support for access to trade finance and SCF	INO	80.2%
	LAO	46.2%
	PHI	71.0%
	THA	60.1%
Business restructuring fund	INO	80.4%
	LAO	49.6%
	PHI	71.8%
	THA	67.7%
Debtor-in-possession financing	INO	84.6%
	LAO	48.5%
	PHI	54.4%
	THA	46.0%

B. March-April 2021

Measure	Country	Strongly want
Special refinancing/low-interest loans	INO	40.1%
	LAO	47.9%
	PHI	52.3%
	THA	69.6%
Zero-interest/collateral-free loans	INO	49.3%
	LAO	57.4%
	PHI	57.8%
	THA	79.6%
Special credit guarantees	INO	34.0%
	LAO	38.3%
	PHI	47.9%
	THA	59.1%
Faster loan approval (simplified procedures)	INO	42.2%
	LAO	53.2%
	PHI	56.5%
	THA	73.7%
Deferred debt repayments/moratorium	INO	39.8%
	LAO	46.8%
	PHI	45.1%
	THA	60.2%
Debt restructuring	INO	35.4%
	LAO	42.6%
	PHI	45.5%
	THA	60.7%
Facilitating access to new financing models (DFS)	INO	22.0%
	LAO	44.7%
	PHI	46.2%
	THA	59.2%
Support for access to trade finance and SCF	INO	33.5%
	LAO	42.6%
	PHI	51.6%
	THA	58.7%
Business restructuring fund	INO	28.9%
	LAO	34.0%
	PHI	48.2%
	THA	64.1%
Debtor-in-possession financing	INO	29.7%
	LAO	43.6%
	PHI	40.5%
	THA	43.2%

Legend: ■ Strongly want ■ Somewhat want

DFS = digital financial services; INO = Indonesia; LAO = Lao People's Democratic Republic (Lao PDR); MSME = micro, small, and medium-sized enterprise; PHI = Philippines; SCF = supply chain finance; THA = Thailand.

Note: For INO, 525 valid samples in March–April 2020 and 2,509 in March–April 2021; For LAO, 355 valid samples in March–April 2020 and 94 in March–April 2021; For PHI, 1,804 valid samples in March–April 2020 and 1,546 in March–April 2021; For THA, 1,147 valid samples in March–April 2020 and 963 in March–April 2021.

Source: Calculated based on MSME surveys in Indonesia, the Lao PDR, the Philippines, and Thailand, March–April 2020–2021.

In Thailand, zero-interest/collateral-free loans (90.2%) ranked first in 2020, followed by faster loan approvals (86.7%) and assistance from a business restructuring fund (84.2%). In 2021, the top three were all about access to credit (90.3% for zero-interest/collateral-free loans, 86.7% for faster loan approval, and 85.7% for refinance/low-interest loans). Similar to Indonesia, at the start of the pandemic in 2020, most MSMEs were pessimistic about their business; they likely considered bankruptcy and sought assistance to restructure their business.

Figure 17 shows MSME responses to nonfinance-related policy measures, also using answers "strongly needed" and "somewhat needed." The subsidy programs/cash transfer/grants for business recovery and the tax relief/corporate tax reduction remained the two top-ranked policy measures MSMEs desired in both the March–April 2020 and March–April 2021 surveys. Their desired nonfinance policy support measures also slightly differed by country.

In Indonesia, subsidy/cash transfer/grants for business recovery (93.7%) was the most desired measure in 2020, followed by a comprehensive information platform on government assistance programs (89.3%) and business development and advisory services (85.1%). In 2021, subsidy/cash transfer/grants for business recovery (81.4%)

remained the most desired, followed by support in upgrading worker skills (77.5%) and business development and advisory services (75.2%). When the pandemic began in 2020, most MSMEs lacked information on what government assistance programs were available, which likely contributed to an increase of pessimism on business (going bankrupt) among MSME owners and managers. MSMEs surveyed in 2021 continued to seek government support for strengthening their businesses and training employees.

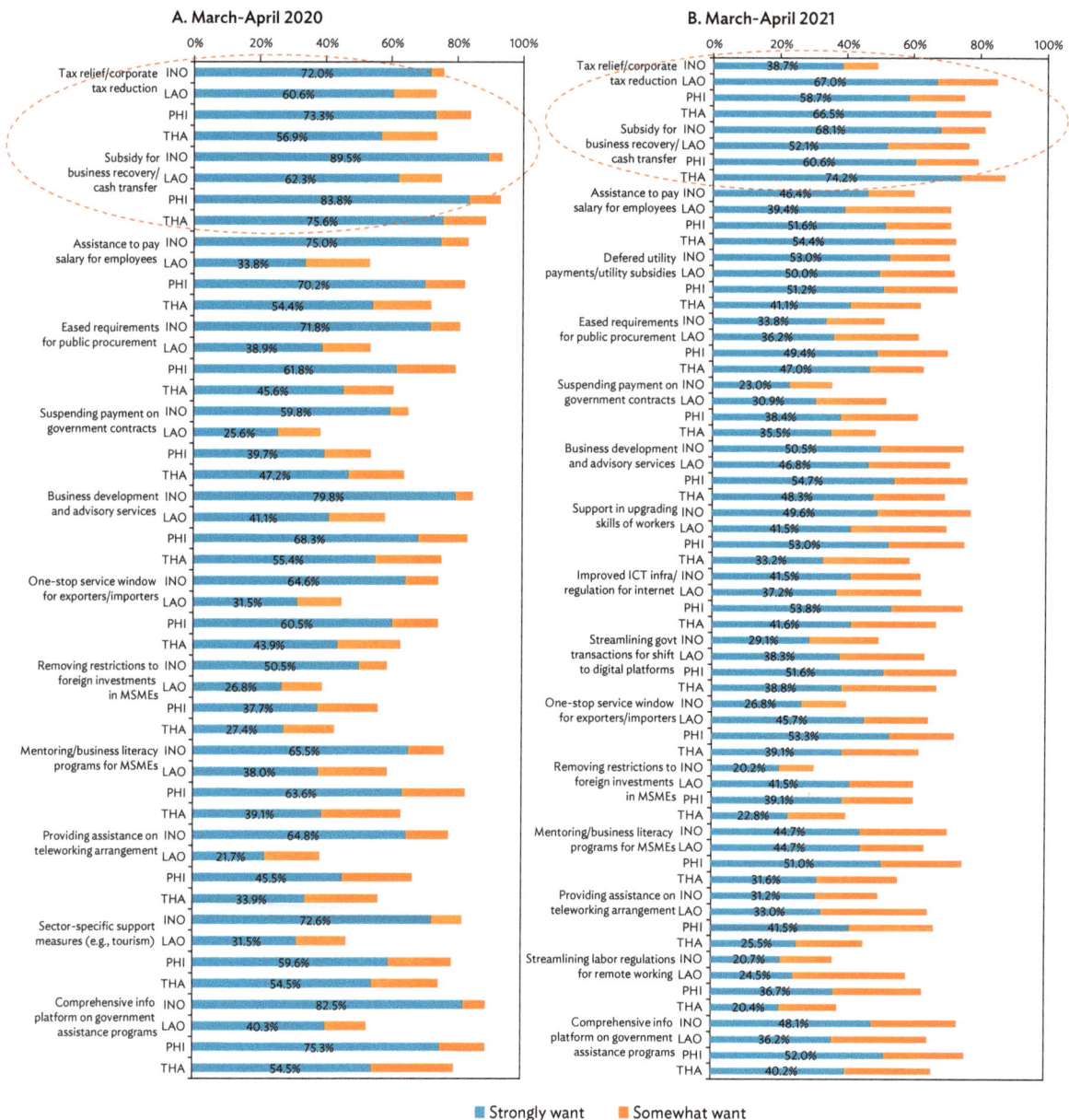

Figure 17: Nonfinancial Policy Measures Desired by MSMEs, 2020–2021

ICT = information and communications technology; INO = Indonesia; LAO = Lao People's Democratic Republic (Lao PDR); MSME = micro, small, and medium-sized enterprise; PHI = Philippines; THA = Thailand.

Note: For INO, 525 valid samples in March–April 2020 and 2,509 in March–April 2021; For LAO, 355 valid samples in March–April 2020 and 94 in March–April 2021; For PHI, 1,804 valid samples in March–April 2020 and 1,546 in March–April 2021; For THA, 1,147 valid samples in March–April 2020 and 963 in March–April 2021.

Source: Calculated based on MSME surveys in Indonesia, the Lao PDR, the Philippines, and Thailand, March–April 2020–2021.

In the Lao PDR, subsidy/cash transfer/grants for business recovery (75.2%) also topped the wish list in 2020, followed by tax relief/corporate tax reduction (73.5%) and mentoring/business literacy programs for MSMEs (59.2%). In 2021, tax relief/corporate tax reduction (85.1%) ranked first, followed by subsidy/cash transfer/grants for business recovery (76.6%) and deferred utility payments/utility subsidies (72.3%). Into 2021, work-from-home arrangements for MSMEs likely increased electricity costs, seeking some assistance for covering their utility costs.

In the Philippines, subsidy/cash transfer/grants for business recovery (93.3%) also ranked first in 2020, followed by a comprehensive information platform on government assistance programs (89.2%) and tax relief/corporate tax reduction (84.1%). In 2021, subsidy/cash transfer/grants for business recovery (79.4%) remained on top, followed by business development and advisory services (76.5%) and a comprehensive information platform on government assistance programs (76.1%). A year into the pandemic, MSMEs sought more information on available government assistance.

In Thailand, subsidy/cash transfer/grants for business recovery (88.8%) ranked first in 2020, followed by a comprehensive information platform on government assistance programs (79.7%) and business development and advisory services (75.5%). In 2021, subsidy/cash transfer/grants for business recovery (87.5%) remained at the top, followed by tax relief/corporate tax reduction (83.1%) and assistance to pay salaries for employees (72.8%). Similar to Indonesia, at the start of the pandemic, most MSMEs lacked information on government assistance programs, which may also have contributed to their pessimistic outlook on business (going bankrupt). Those surveyed in 2021 likely prioritized internal cost management (wage payments) to overcome the poor business environment caused by the pandemic and social restrictions.

3.   Post-Pandemic Policy Actions

It is quite likely that the policies taken by the four countries were successful in promoting economic recovery in 2021 from the 2020 growth contractions. Governments offered a wide range of support measures seamlessly to individuals, households, businesses, and their workers, as they imposed social restrictions and lockdowns to contain new COVID-19 infections. The policies clearly dented national budgets. The highest concern for continuing the recovery is how to secure the sizable long-term funds needed to continue to provide sustainable assistance to people and businesses. Uncertainty over when COVID-19 will be contained remains, given the prospect of new coronavirus variants or just learning to live with the virus.

Strengthening the development of MSMEs and their dynamism is critical to boost national productivity, create jobs, and drive resilient growth across developing Asia. The pandemic damaged most MSMEs. They will require continuous government support to maintain operations and grow, and governments will continue to support them as MSMEs remain a key driver for a sustainable and resilient recovery from the pandemic. Given the continuing pandemic, it is critical to rethink how to best fund sustainable delivery of government assistance to MSMEs or build innovative and effective long-term support for MSMEs. To this end, governments will need to design MSME development policies in two stages: (i) policies during a continuing pandemic and (ii) post-pandemic policies. Understanding how MSMEs made it through the first year of the pandemic is an important first step in creating a feasible framework for post-pandemic policy actions effectively using limited national budgets.

This study provides evidence on MSME business conditions a year into the pandemic. The ADB surveys showed that the business environment improved moderately with many MSMEs reopening their business into 2021. But domestic demand for MSME products and services had not recovered fully as of March–April 2021. As the pandemic prolonged, two streams of businesses were created and expanded: MSMEs that were hit hard by the pandemic and those that benefited from the pandemic and social restrictions, although the latter remained a small fraction. Those who reported better business conditions were mostly firms supplying essential daily goods and services including food and health-care products. The hardest-hit MSMEs were typically those dealing in nonessential goods and services. This corresponded to the revenue structure of MSMEs. The pandemic and social restrictions split MSMEs into those profitable and less profitable, creating inequality in business performance.

In general, employment by MSMEs improved into 2021, with reduced layoffs and wage payment cuts. Instead, worker options expanded—including work-from-home (teleworking), reduced working hours, and granted leaves. In 2021, MSMEs that managed their employees well (good internal control) likely increased. Financial conditions also improved among MSMEs, with fewer with little access to cash or funding, increasing those with enough short-term cash/funding to maintain operations. Most MSMEs continued to rely on informal financing and their own funds during the pandemic. But supported by large government financial assistance, their access to bank credit improved markedly; it generated further demand for government funding support among MSMEs. During the first year of the pandemic, digital financial services were not a widely available funding option for them.

The study also broke down its analyses into specific groups. The prolonged pandemic and frequently adopted government mobility restrictions decimated tourism across countries. Accordingly, tourism-related MSMEs—including restaurants, hotels, tour services, transportation services, and souvenir shops—continued to face a harsh business environment a year into the pandemic. Large income losses remained among them, despite government support measures like travel incentive programs. With tourism performance highly dependent on the extent of mobility restrictions, the industry will continue to face difficulties until COVID-19 is contained.

Digitalization accelerated during the pandemic, with digitally operated MSMEs growing in number, adjusting their traditional personal-contact-based business into e-commerce. This digital transformation will only expand, particularly if there are frequent national mobility restrictions as new variants appear. However, digitally operated MSMEs were not always successful during the survey periods. Among them, two streams of business clusters were also created and expanded: those that were profitable and those less profitable. Those profitable dealt mainly in essential goods and services, including delivery services, with those unprofitable mainly in nonessential goods and services. Some reasons for non-profitable digital businesses include the limited demand on nonessential goods and services during the pandemic and social restrictions, unorganized business models that lacked good strategies before starting, unfamiliarity with the use of technology in operations, and failed initial cost management when digitalizing operations. The digital transformation is a priority agenda for post-pandemic policies across countries. Given the scant use of digital financial services even among digitally operated firms during the pandemic, a digitalization policy framework should be combined with promoting digital financial services that improve firm's internal cost management.

Women-led MSMEs—those run or owned by women—had mixed business outcomes during the pandemic. They were also split into two groups: those hurt by the pandemic and social restrictions and those enjoying a better business environment than before the pandemic. The latter was a small fraction, but women-led MSMEs with higher revenues were also likely involved in digital operations.

Like tourism-related MSMEs, internationalized MSMEs—those involved in the global supply chains or export/import business—faced a harsh business environment 1 year into the pandemic. They were directly affected by lockdowns and frequent mobility restrictions, faced severe supply chain disruptions and contract cancellations. In 2021, economies gradually moved into the recovery stage as consumption and exports revived. But the trickle-down effect from the economic recovery had yet to materialize for internationalized MSMEs at the time the surveys were conducted. However, like women-led MSMEs, two streams of business groups come out and expanded: those severely damaged by the pandemic and social restrictions and those which were able to manage the COVID-19 shocks better. The latter was a small fraction, but many operated digitally. Again, digitalization policies should cover both women-led and internationalized MSMEs.

Finance was a top concern for MSMEs surveyed a year into the pandemic. They continued to struggle to reduce costs, including further layoffs in the future, to maintain business. As they learn to live with COVID-19, MSMEs will need to apply smarter cost management. This is one reason why digitalizing MSME operations and administration is a potential solution. The ADB surveys also found that MSMEs surveyed expected further government support for access to finance, subsidy programs, and tax relief. They also sought timely information about government assistance programs. They intended to strengthen their business resiliency against shocks like COVID-19, asking government to provide business development and advisory services and skills development training for workers.

Considering the findings from the ADB surveys and the analysis, MSME development policies should be well designed with an "exit" strategy from the pandemic in two stages—those with COVID-19 (on-pandemic policies) and without COVID-19 (post-pandemic policies). Some high-level policy implications include the following:

A.   On-pandemic policies for MSME development

- **Provide timely information on government support programs.**

    A lesson from the first rapid surveys suggested that a lack of information on government assistance programs contributed to business pessimism (going bankrupt) among MSMEs. Given the high mobile phone penetration in countries surveyed, building a mobile information portal on government assistance programs would be worth considering.

- **Build focused group assistance proportionately.**

    The surveys found that two streams of business groups appeared and expanded during the pandemic: MSMEs hit hard by the pandemic and social restrictions and those which benefited, although there were far less that benefited. This was true for digitally operated MSMEs, women-led MSMEs, and internationalized MSMEs. Thus, assistance should be allocated more to those adversely affected proportionately to the impact level.

- **Create a phased approach for assistance with well-scheduled budget allocations.**

    As the pandemic continues, the risk of bloating national budgets will increase. Governments will need to secure sufficient financing to provide sustainable support programs over the long term, in a phased manner within a well-controlled budget framework.

- **Promote the digital transformation and the use of technology for business.**

    The digital transformation brings several benefits to MSMEs. It enhances access to business information, strengthens business networks, creates new business opportunities (including access to global marketplaces and global supply chains), and reduces administrative costs. However, digital operations did not always lead to successful business operations during the pandemic. The surveys found the business environment of firms dealing in nonessential goods and services remained severe even if they were digitalized. Some transformed their business into online selling during the pandemic, but those with a premature business model that lacks strategy failed. MSMEs need comprehensive assistance for digitalization, including guidance on developing e-commerce, online administrative and cost management, and funding by digital financial services.

B.   Post-pandemic policies for MSME development

The following actions can also begin during the on-pandemic period. These post-pandemic policies focus more on the "growth" of MSMEs to boost national productivity and create more quality jobs. They enhance MSME dynamism to help build a sustainable and resilient recovery from the pandemic.

- **Provide business development services and skills development training for workers.**

  A drop in domestic demand over the years of the pandemic is an issue to improve for MSMEs. Strengthening business competitiveness is critical for creating new demand, to survive and grow during a post-pandemic recovery. Business development and advisory services and training for workers' skill upgrades are critical areas. These also help create a base of quality jobs nationwide.

- **Foster incubators and accelerators for entrepreneurship development.**

  Business incubators and accelerators play an important role in enhancing MSME competitiveness and developing entrepreneurship. It is critical to foster more incubators and accelerators to create a base of growth-oriented MSMEs and innovative startups nationally.

- **Provide more growth capital for business by diversifying alternative financing options.**

  Finance is critical to maintain business and grow. During the pandemic, working capital financing is a lifeline to continue business or maintain the status quo. After the pandemic, more diversified financing options are needed for MSMEs to meet their financing needs. The assistance should include further promotion of digital financial services for MSMEs (such as mobile financing, peer-to-peer lending, and equity crowdfunding platforms) and developing MSME equity markets as a growth capital financing venue for growing MSMEs and emerging businesses.

- **Use more private sector resources for policy implementation.**

  It is crucial for governments to attract private sector support to implement policy goals on MSME development. Outsourcing financial and business administration of MSMEs—for example, using advisory professionals such as certified public accountants to strengthen the internal control system of the MSME—would be worth considering.

Conclusion

This report examined how Asia's small businesses survived 1 year into the COVID-19 pandemic and what policy actions would be needed to revitalize them post-pandemic, based on descriptive analysis using unweighted data in Indonesia, the Lao PDR, the Philippines, and Thailand. Due to the urgency of capturing MSME conditions to help design policies for MSMEs during the pandemic, the study used online surveys (nonstandard sampling procedures). As a result, survey respondents formed different groups at respective data points (March-April 2020, August-September 2020, and March-April 2021). Nonetheless, it is meaningful that the analysis focused on the change in respondents within the same group of MSMEs 1 year into the pandemic. The analysis suggested that MSMEs surveyed in 2020 might have gone out of business, while those resilient to the COVID-19 crisis continued into 2021.

Overall, the business environment of MSMEs improved 1 year after the pandemic began in March 2020, but many continued to face limited demand. As lessons, firms' ability to withstand the pandemic impact differed by type of business and operations. Hence, assistance should continue for those adversely affected as targeted groups with measures proportionate to each impact level. Tourism-related MSMEs, digitally operated MSMEs, women-led MSMEs, and internationalized MSMEs should be included in these focused groups. Given the continuing pandemic and increased risks of bloating national budgets, a phased approach for government assistance should be done under a well-controlled budget framework. The ADB surveys showed that working-capital shortages were another concern for MSME survival during and after the pandemic. Aside from this, more growth capital should be made available to businesses with high growth potential, startups, and entrepreneurs. This will help governments achieve a more resilient post-pandemic economic recovery. The digital transformation brings several benefits to MSMEs and entrepreneurs. The pandemic triggered many MSMEs to go digital, but their digital operations were not always successful due mainly to premature business models that lacked long-term strategies. The assistance should include guidance on e-commerce development and the use of technology for new business.

Lastly, the continuous monitoring of MSME business conditions is crucial for governments to design and implement feasible evidence-based policies. Support for national monitoring and evaluation efforts is one of the key missions of the ADB Asia SME Monitor project.

Comparison between ADB Surveys and National Statistics Distributions

A. Indonesia

Item	ADB Survey, March–April 2020 (Employment Grouping)				ADB Survey, August–September 2020 (Employment Grouping)				ADB Survey, March–April 2021 (Employment Grouping)				BPS 2016 Economic Census (Employment Grouping)				Difference between ADB and BPS Distribution (%)		
	Micro and Small	Medium and Large	Total	Share (%)	Micro and Small	Medium and Large	Total	Share (%)	Micro and Small	Medium and Large	Total	Share (%)	Micro and Small	Medium and Large	Total	Share (%)	March–April 2020	August–September 2020	March–April 2021
By industrial sector, total	465	14	479	100.0	114	2	116	100.0	2,377	51	2,428	100.0	26,073,689	348,567	26,422,256	100.0	–	–	–
Mining and quarrying	–	–	–	–	–	–	–	–	1	–	1	0.0	170,004	1,778	171,782	0.7	(0.7)	(0.7)	(0.6)
Manufacturing	30	3	33	6.9	11	1	12	10.3	89	7	96	4.0	4,348,459	35,163	4,383,622	16.6	(9.7)	(6.2)	(12.6)
Electricity, gas, steam and air-conditioning supply	1	–	1	0.2	–	–	–	–	10	–	10	0.4	29,928	1,292	31,220	0.1	0.1	(0.1)	0.3
Water supply; sewerage, waste management and remediation activities	4	–	4	0.8	4	–	4	3.4	25	1	26	1.1	91,541	1,317	92,858	0.4	0.5	3.1	0.7
Construction	24	–	24	5.0	1	–	1	0.9	9	1	10	0.4	225,795	27,868	253,663	1.0	4.1	(0.1)	(0.5)
Wholesale and retail trade; repair of motor vehicles and motorcycles	226	4	230	48.0	27	–	27	23.3	960	10	970	40.0	12,097,326	157,868	12,255,194	46.4	1.6	(23.1)	(6.4)
Transport and storage	8	–	8	1.7	1	–	1	0.9	11	2	13	0.5	1,281,250	21,205	1,302,455	4.9	(3.3)	(4.1)	(4.4)
Accommodation and food service activities	95	2	97	20.3	35	1	36	31.0	764	7	771	31.8	4,431,154	16,093	4,447,247	16.8	3.4	14.2	14.9
Information and communication	7	–	7	1.5	3	–	3	2.6	28	2	30	1.2	625,772	8,133	633,905	2.4	(0.9)	0.2	(1.2)
Financial and insurance activities	6	1	7	1.5	1	–	1	0.9	3	5	8	0.3	86,266	28,379	114,645	0.4	1.0	0.4	(0.1)
Real estate activities	–	–	–	–	–	–	–	–	3	–	3	0.1	385,491	6,509	392,000	1.5	(1.5)	(1.5)	(1.4)
Professional, scientific, and technical activities	11	–	11	2.3	10	–	10	8.6	81	5	86	3.5	352,936	24,004	376,940	1.4	0.9	7.2	2.1
Administrative and support service activities	13	–	13	2.7	–	–	–	–	–	–	–	–	–	–	–	–	2.7	–	–
Public administration and defense; compulsory social security	–	–	–	–	–	–	–	–	1	–	1	0.0	–	–	–	–	–	–	0.0
Education	4	2	6	1.3	–	–	–	–	24	2	26	1.1	590,423	8,362	598,785	2.3	(1.0)	(2.3)	(1.2)
Human health and social work activities	2	1	3	0.6	2	–	2	1.7	14	–	14	0.6	209,048	3,781	212,829	0.8	(0.2)	0.9	(0.2)
Arts, entertainment, and recreation	6	–	6	1.3	–	–	–	–	–	–	–	–	–	–	–	–	1.3	–	–
Other service activities	28	1	29	6.1	19	–	19	16.4	354	9	363	15.0	1,148,296	6,815	1,155,111	4.4	1.7	12.0	10.6
By province, total	465	14	479	100.0	114	2	116	100.0	2,377	51	2,428	100.0	26,073,689	348,567	26,422,256	100.0	–	–	–
Aceh	7	–	7	1.5	–	–	–	–	8	–	8	0.3	422,469	4,412	426,881	1.6	(0.2)	(1.6)	(1.3)
Bali	29	3	32	6.7	–	–	–	–	5	1	6	0.2	464,787	10,112	474,899	1.8	4.9	(1.8)	(1.6)
Banten	12	1	13	2.7	5	–	5	4.3	45	4	49	2.0	943,922	20,630	964,552	3.7	(0.9)	0.7	(1.6)
Bengkulu	2	–	2	0.4	1	–	1	0.9	1	–	1	0.0	195,775	1,859	197,634	0.7	(0.3)	0.1	(0.7)

Item	ADB Survey, March–April 2020 Employment Grouping				ADB Survey, August–September 2020 Employment Grouping				ADB Survey, March–April 2021 Employment Grouping				BPS 2016 Economic Census Employment Grouping				Difference between ADB and BPS Distribution (%)		
	Micro and Small	Medium and Large	Total	Share (%)	Micro and Small	Medium and Large	Total	Share (%)	Micro and Small	Medium and Large	Total	Share (%)	Micro and Small	Medium and Large	Total	Share (%)	March–April 2020	August–September 2020	March–April 2021
DI Yogyakarta	35	1	36	7.5	2	–	2	1.7	12	–	12	0.5	521,011	6,744	527,755	2.0	5.5	(0.3)	(1.5)
DKI Jakarta	35	1	36	7.5	5	–	5	4.3	284	7	291	12.0	1,151,080	63,340	1,214,420	4.6	2.9	(0.3)	7.4
Gorontalo	2	–	2	0.4	–	–	–	–	–	–	–	–	156,935	823	157,758	0.6	(0.2)	(0.6)	(0.6)
Jambi	4	–	4	0.8	1	–	1	0.9	1	–	1	0.0	310,775	3,462	314,237	1.2	(0.4)	(0.3)	(1.1)
Jawa Barat	78	–	78	16.3	22	2	24	20.7	807	24	831	34.2	4,545,874	53,373	4,599,247	17.4	(1.1)	3.3	16.8
Jawa Tengah	53	1	54	11.3	13	–	13	11.2	34	1	35	1.4	4,105,917	33,673	4,139,590	15.7	(4.4)	(4.5)	(14.2)
Jawa Timur	60	3	63	13.2	43	–	43	37.1	504	10	514	21.2	4,569,822	48,461	4,618,283	17.5	(4.3)	19.6	3.7
Kalimantan Barat	10	–	10	2.1	1	–	1	0.9	3	–	3	0.1	292,705	4,540	297,245	1.1	1.0	(0.3)	(1.0)
Kalimantan Selatan	4	–	4	0.8	1	–	1	0.9	53	–	53	2.2	461,762	4,610	466,372	1.8	(0.9)	(0.9)	0.4
Kalimantan Tengah	6	–	6	1.3	–	–	–	–	4	–	4	0.2	231,123	3,016	234,139	0.9	0.4	(0.9)	(0.7)
Kalimantan Timur	10	–	10	2.1	1	–	1	0.9	–	–	–	–	299,910	7,328	307,238	1.2	0.9	(0.3)	(1.2)
Kalimantan Utara	–	–	–	–	–	–	–	–	36	–	36	1.5	51,844	1,008	52,852	0.2	(0.2)	(0.2)	1.3
Kep. Bangka Belitung	3	–	3	0.6	1	–	1	0.9	–	–	–	–	124,721	1,590	126,311	0.5	0.1	0.4	(0.5)
Kepulauan Riau	4	–	4	0.8	2	–	2	1.7	–	–	–	–	146,638	6,353	152,991	0.6	0.3	1.1	(0.6)
Lampung	7	1	8	1.7	–	–	–	–	2	–	2	0.1	770,632	6,428	777,060	2.9	(1.3)	(2.9)	(2.9)
Maluku	–	–	–	–	–	–	–	–	–	–	–	–	147,698	1,271	148,969	0.6	(0.6)	(0.6)	(0.6)
Maluku Utara	–	–	–	–	1	–	1	0.9	–	–	–	–	80,219	940	81,159	0.3	(0.3)	0.6	(0.3)
Nusa Tenggara Barat	3	–	3	0.6	–	–	–	–	14	–	14	0.6	580,168	3,807	583,975	2.2	(1.6)	(2.2)	(1.6)
Nusa Tenggara Timur	5	–	5	1.0	2	–	2	1.7	1	–	1	0.0	430,312	2,361	432,673	1.6	(0.6)	0.1	(1.6)
Papua	5	–	5	1.0	–	–	–	–	–	–	–	–	148,647	2,823	151,470	0.6	0.5	(0.6)	(0.6)
Papua Barat	2	–	2	0.4	–	–	–	–	–	–	–	–	71,803	1,441	73,244	0.3	0.1	(0.3)	(0.3)
Riau	4	–	4	0.8	–	–	–	–	4	–	4	0.2	509,252	8,854	518,106	2.0	(1.1)	(2.0)	(1.8)
Sulawesi Barat	1	–	1	0.2	–	–	–	–	–	–	–	–	135,355	669	136,024	0.5	(0.3)	(0.5)	(0.5)
Sulawesi Selatan	12	1	13	2.7	1	–	1	0.9	5	–	5	0.2	914,871	10,177	925,048	3.5	(0.8)	(2.6)	(3.3)
Sulawesi Tengah	2	–	2	0.4	1	–	1	0.9	–	–	–	–	337,905	2,635	340,540	1.3	(0.9)	(0.4)	(1.3)
Sulawesi Tenggara	3	–	3	0.6	–	–	–	–	1	–	1	0.0	279,421	2,419	281,840	1.1	(0.4)	(1.1)	(1.0)
Sulawesi Utara	21	–	21	4.4	2	–	2	1.7	26	1	27	1.1	292,122	3,108	295,230	1.1	3.3	0.6	(0.0)
Sumatera Barat	11	–	11	2.3	–	–	–	–	2	–	2	0.1	580,344	6,590	586,934	2.2	0.1	(2.2)	(2.1)
Sumatera Selatan	7	–	7	1.5	5	–	5	4.3	–	–	–	–	644,112	6,550	650,662	2.5	(1.0)	1.8	(2.5)
Sumatera Utara	28	2	30	6.3	4	–	4	3.4	525	3	528	21.7	1,153,758	13,160	1,166,918	4.4	1.8	(1.0)	17.3

ADB = Asian Development Bank; BPS = Badan Pusat Statistik (Statistics Office in Indonesia); COVID-19 = coronavirus disease; MSME = micro, small, and medium-sized enterprise.

Notes: ADB survey data has complete responses from agriculture (49 out of 528 complete samples in March–April 2020, 13 out of 129 in August–September 2020, and 87 out of 2,515 in March–April 2021). As agriculture is not included in the industrial classification of BPS statistics on MSMEs, the distribution of ADB survey data refer to the distribution of BPS statistics, excluding agriculture, for the purpose of comparison. Enterprise classification refers to the employment threshold set by BPS.

Sources: ADB Indonesia MSME Surveys on COVID-19 Impact (March–April 2020, August–September 2020, and March–April 2021) and BPS 2016 Economic Census.

B. Lao People's Democratic Republic (Lao PDR)

Item	ADB Survey, March–April 2020 Employment Grouping						ADB Survey, March–April 2021 Employment Grouping						DERM Enterprise Database (as of 3 June 2020) Employment Grouping						Difference between ADB and DERM Distribution (%)	
	Micro	Small	Medium	Large	Total	Share (%)	Micro	Small	Medium	Large	Total	Share (%)	Micro	Small	Medium	Large	Total	Share (%)	March–April 2020	March–April 2021
By industrial sector, total	206	137	12	7	362	100	48	38	8	3	97	100	–	–	–	–	212,290	100.0		
Agriculture, forestry, and fishing	14	12	2	1	29	8.0	2	1	–	–	3	3.1	–	–	–	–	9,702	4.6	3.4	(1.5)
Mining and quarrying	2	–	–	–	2	0.6	–	–	–	–	–	–	–	–	–	–	2,054	1.0	(0.4)	(1.0)
Manufacturing	20	27	4	2	53	14.6	4	1	1	–	6	6.2	–	–	–	–	21,821	10.3	4.4	(4.1)
Electricity, gas, steam and air-conditioning supply	4	1	–	–	5	1.4	–	–	–	–	–	–	–	–	–	–	–	–	1.4	–
Water supply; sewerage, waste management and remediation activities	1	–	–	–	1	0.3	–	–	–	–	–	–	–	–	–	–	–	–	0.3	–
Construction	3	10	–	–	13	3.6	–	2	–	–	2	2.1	–	–	–	–	5,693	2.7	0.9	(0.6)
Wholesale and retail trade; repair of motor vehicles and motorcycles	80	17	1	1	99	27.3	25	14	4	2	45	46.4	–	–	–	–	98,525	46.4	(19.1)	(0.0)
Transport and storage	8	8	–	–	16	4.4	1	–	–	–	1	1.0	–	–	–	–	30,465	14.4	(9.9)	(13.3)
Accommodation and food service activities	30	18	1	1	50	13.8	2	3	–	–	5	5.2	–	–	–	–	15,038	7.1	6.7	(1.9)
Information and communication	4	3	–	–	7	1.9	2	–	–	–	2	2.1	–	–	–	–	3,137	1.5	0.5	0.6
Financial and insurance activities	2	9	–	–	11	3.0	2	8	2	1	13	13.4	–	–	–	–	1,162	0.5	2.5	12.9
Real estate activities	1	–	–	–	1	0.3	–	–	–	–	–	–	–	–	–	–	1,394	0.7	(0.4)	(0.7)
Professional, scientific, and technical activities	4	1	–	–	5	1.4	2	1	–	–	3	3.1	–	–	–	–	3,009	1.4	(0.0)	1.7
Administrative and support service activities	20	10	1	–	31	8.6	1	3	–	–	4	4.1	–	–	–	–	5,039	2.4	6.2	1.8
Public administration and defense; compulsory social security	6	18	3	2	29	8.0	–	–	–	–	–	–	–	–	–	–	1,771	0.8	7.2	(0.8)
Education	4	–	–	–	4	1.1	–	2	–	–	2	2.1	–	–	–	–	1,031	0.5	0.6	1.6
Human health and social work activities	–	1	–	–	1	0.3	–	–	–	–	–	–	–	–	–	–	1,730	0.8	(0.5)	(0.8)
Arts, entertainment, and recreation	3	2	–	–	5	1.4	1	–	–	–	1	1.0	–	–	–	–	10,018	4.7	(3.3)	(3.7)
Other service activities	–	–	–	–	–	–	6	3	1	–	10	10.3	–	–	–	–	701	0.3	(0.3)	10.0
By province, total	206	137	12	7	362	100.0	48	38	8	3	97	100.0	–	–	–	–	176,182	100.0		
Attapeu	1	–	–	–	1	0.3	–	–	–	–	–	–	–	–	–	–	2,429	1.4	(1.1)	(1.4)
Bokeo	1	1	–	–	2	0.6	–	–	–	–	–	–	–	–	–	–	6,153	3.5	(2.9)	(3.5)

Item	ADB Survey, March–April 2020 Employment Grouping						ADB Survey, March–April 2021 Employment Grouping						DERM Enterprise Database (as of 3 June 2020) Employment Grouping						Difference between ADB and DERM Distribution (%)	
	Micro	Small	Medium	Large	Total	Share (%)	Micro	Small	Medium	Large	Total	Share (%)	Micro	Small	Medium	Large	Total	Share (%)	March–April 2020	March–April 2021
Bolikhamsai/Bolikhamxay	5	4	–	–	9	2.5	1	3	–	–	4	4.1	–	–	–	–	7,164	4.1	(1.6)	0.1
Champasak (Champasack)	9	4	1	3	17	4.7	1	1	–	–	2	2.1	–	–	–	–	14,419	8.2	(3.5)	(6.1)
Hua Phan	8	2	–	–	10	2.8	–	1	–	–	1	1.0	–	–	–	–	5,858	3.3	(0.6)	(2.3)
Khammouane	5	9	–	–	14	3.9	3	–	–	–	3	3.1	–	–	–	–	6,203	3.5	0.3	(0.4)
Luang Namtha	3	1	–	–	4	1.1	3	1	–	–	4	4.1	–	–	–	–	3,881	2.2	(1.1)	1.9
Luang Prabang	16	14	1	–	31	8.6	1	2	1	–	4	4.1	–	–	–	–	16,180	9.2	(0.6)	(5.1)
Oudomxay	1	1	–	–	2	0.6	–	–	1	–	1	1.0	–	–	–	–	5,815	3.3	(2.7)	(2.3)
Phongsali (Phongsaly)	25	6	1	–	32	8.8	–	–	–	–	–	–	–	–	–	–	2,571	1.5	7.4	(1.5)
Sayabouly (Xayabury)	2	6	1	–	9	2.5	–	–	–	–	–	–	–	–	–	–	11,102	6.3	(3.8)	(6.3)
Salavan (Saravane)	5	1	–	–	6	1.7	–	–	–	–	–	–	–	–	–	–	5,273	3.0	(1.3)	(3.0)
Savannakhet	3	6	–	–	9	2.5	1	1	–	–	2	2.1	–	–	–	–	9,387	5.3	(2.8)	(3.3)
Sekong	3	2	–	–	5	1.4	–	–	–	–	–	–	–	–	–	–	1,626	0.9	0.5	(0.9)
Vientiane Prefecture	89	67	7	4	167	46.1	24	27	6	3	60	61.9	–	–	–	–	53,173	30.2	16.0	31.7
Vientiane Province	11	6	1	–	18	5.0	5	–	–	–	5	5.2	–	–	–	–	14,133	8.0	(3.0)	(2.9)
Xieng Khouang (Xiengkhuang)	16	6	–	–	22	6.1	9	2	–	–	11	11.3	–	–	–	–	8,866	5.0	1.0	6.3
Xaisomboun (Xaysomboun)	3	1	–	–	4	1.1	–	–	–	–	–	–	–	–	–	–	1,949	1.1	(0.0)	(1.1)

ADB = Asian Development Bank; COVID-19 = coronavirus disease; DERM = Department of Enterprise Registration and Management, Ministry of Industry and Commerce; MSME = micro, small, and medium-sized enterprise.

Sources: ADB Lao PDR MSME Surveys on COVID-19 Impact (March–April 2020 and March–April 2021) and DERM enterprise database as of 3 June 2020. Employment-based classification.

C. Philippines

Item	ADB Survey, March–April 2020 (Employment Grouping) Micro	Small	Medium	Large	Total	Share (%)	ADB Survey, August–September 2020 (Employment Grouping) Micro	Small	Medium	Large	Total	Share (%)	ADB Survey, March–April 2021 (Employment Grouping) Micro	Small	Medium	Large	Total	Share (%)	PSA List of Establishments, 2018 (Employment Grouping) Micro	Small	Medium	Large	Total	Share (%)	Difference between ADB and PSA Distribution (%) March–April 2020	August–September 2020	March–April 2021
By industrial sector, total	1,461	318	25	16	1,820	100	613	64	9	7	693	100	1,357	169	20	60	1,606	100	887,272	106,175	4,895	4,769	1,003,111	100.0	–	–	–
Agriculture, forestry, and fishing	79	18	2	2	101	5.5	40	4	–	2	46	6.6	94	17	–	2	113	7.0	5,837	2,512	157	173	8,679	0.9	4.7	5.8	6.2
Mining and quarrying	–	–	–	–	–	–	–	1	–	–	1	0.1	–	–	–	–	–	–	492	302	21	35	850	0.1	(0.1)	0.1	(0.1)
Manufacturing	458	111	6	2	577	31.7	172	17	1	–	190	27.4	282	53	11	16	362	22.5	103,590	11,678	1,067	1,133	117,468	11.7	20.0	15.7	10.8
Electricity, gas, steam and air-conditioning supply	11	1	1	–	13	0.7	5	–	–	–	5	0.7	8	1	–	–	9	0.6	478	633	98	89	1,298	0.1	0.6	0.6	0.4
Water supply; sewerage, waste management and remediation activities	–	–	–	–	–	–	5	–	–	–	5	0.7	5	2	–	–	7	0.4	677	711	49	29	1,466	0.1	(0.1)	0.6	0.3
Construction	36	15	3	2	56	3.1	11	2	–	–	13	1.9	23	7	–	1	31	1.9	2,304	1,775	226	262	4,507	0.4	2.6	1.4	1.5
Wholesale and retail trade; repair of motor vehicles and motorcycles	393	55	1	4	453	24.9	140	8	3	–	151	21.8	522	17	1	4	544	33.9	427,101	33,577	1,087	584	462,349	46.1	(21.2)	(24.3)	(12.2)
Transport and storage	21	6	–	–	27	1.5	3	2	–	–	5	0.7	8	6	–	1	15	0.9	7,264	3,511	231	194	11,200	1.1	0.4	(0.4)	(0.2)
Accommodation and food service activities	208	41	4	2	255	14.0	114	16	3	–	133	19.2	154	11	1	1	167	10.4	125,396	18,802	337	105	144,640	14.4	(0.4)	4.8	(4.0)
Information and communication	29	13	1	1	44	2.4	8	1	–	–	9	1.3	13	22	2	18	55	3.4	27,421	1,973	153	140	29,687	3.0	(0.5)	(1.7)	0.5
Financial and insurance activities	6	12	1	–	19	1.0	4	3	1	5	13	1.9	2	5	2	5	14	0.9	37,813	8,053	167	183	46,216	4.6	(3.6)	(2.7)	(3.7)
Real estate activities	11	2	–	–	13	0.7	5	–	–	–	5	0.7	9	–	–	–	9	0.6	9,478	1,975	79	63	11,595	1.2	(0.4)	(0.4)	(0.6)
Professional, scientific, and technical activities	34	9	1	1	45	2.5	7	–	–	–	7	1.0	9	5	1	2	17	1.1	13,617	2,164	104	89	15,974	1.6	0.9	(0.6)	(0.5)
Administrative and support service activities	63	15	1	2	81	4.5	1	–	–	–	1	0.1	10	6	2	7	23	1.4	14,073	3,022	474	1,144	18,713	1.9	2.6	(1.7)	(0.4)
Public administration and defense; compulsory social security	–	–	–	–	–	–	1	–	–	–	1	0.1	–	–	–	–	–	–	–	–	–	–	–	–	–	0.1	–
Education	8	6	3	–	17	0.9	4	2	–	–	6	0.9	5	1	–	1	7	0.4	9,105	8,312	391	271	18,079	1.8	(0.9)	(0.9)	(1.4)
Human health and social work activities	7	1	–	–	8	0.4	9	–	–	–	9	1.3	17	2	–	–	19	1.2	26,076	2,325	200	223	28,824	2.9	(2.4)	(1.6)	(1.7)
Arts, entertainment, and recreation	–	–	–	–	–	–	10	1	–	–	11	1.6	9	2	–	–	11	0.7	13,755	1,563	34	41	15,393	1.5	(1.5)	0.1	(0.8)

Item	ADB Survey, March–April 2020 Employment Grouping						ADB Survey, August–September 2020 Employment Grouping						ADB Survey, March–April 2021 Employment Grouping						PSA List of Establishments, 2018 Employment Grouping						Difference between ADB and PSA Distribution (%)		
	Micro	Small	Medium	Large	Total	Share (%)	Micro	Small	Medium	Large	Total	Share (%)	Micro	Small	Medium	Large	Total	Share (%)	Micro	Small	Medium	Large	Total	Share (%)	March–April 2020	August–September 2020	March–April 2021
Other service activities	97	13	1	–	111	6.1	74	7	1	–	82	11.8	187	12	2	2	203	12.6	62,795	3,347	20	11	66,173	6.6	(0.5)	5.2	6.0
By province, total	1,461	318	25	16	1,820	100.0	613	64	9	7	693	100.0	1,357	169	20	60	1,606	100.0	887,272	106,175	4,895	4,769	1,003,111	100.0			
National Capital Region (NCR)	210	63	5	5	283	15.5	41	25	6	5	77	11.1	44	45	6	32	127	7.9	166,921	34,523	1,868	1,938	205,250	20.5	(4.9)	(9.4)	(12.6)
Cordillera Administrative Region (CAR)	11	5	–	1	17	0.9	5	–	–	–	5	0.7	43	6	2	–	51	3.2	18,783	1,587	47	49	20,466	2.0	(1.1)	(1.3)	1.1
Region I (Ilocos Region)	144	21	1	–	166	9.1	78	6	–	–	84	12.1	17	3	–	–	20	1.2	46,708	3,977	122	70	50,877	5.1	4.0	7.0	(3.8)
Region II (Cagayan Valley)	58	10	–	–	68	3.7	6	–	–	–	6	0.9	479	9	–	2	490	30.5	28,547	2,119	52	35	30,753	3.1	0.7	(2.2)	27.4
Region III (Central Luzon)	128	25	1	2	156	8.6	11	3	–	–	14	2.0	126	14	2	2	144	9.0	104,875	10,754	444	385	116,458	11.6	(3.0)	(9.6)	(2.6)
Region IV-A (CALABARZON)	394	57	3	2	456	25.1	12	4	–	–	16	2.3	46	31	5	12	94	5.9	133,640	13,778	778	811	149,007	14.9	10.2	(12.5)	(9.0)
MIMAROPA Region	41	11	–	–	52	2.9	–	–	–	–	–	–	6	1	–	–	7	0.4	21,948	1,914	57	33	23,952	2.4	0.5	(2.4)	(2.0)
Region V (Bicol Region)	103	16	4	–	123	6.8	–	–	–	1	1	0.1	91	8	–	2	101	6.3	37,111	3,215	118	70	40,514	4.0	2.7	(3.9)	2.3
Region VI (Western Visayas)	33	12	3	–	48	2.6	39	3	1	–	43	6.2	50	7	2	–	59	3.7	55,482	5,894	214	193	61,783	6.2	(3.5)	0.0	(2.5)
Region VII (Central Visayas)	88	41	4	1	134	7.4	2	4	–	–	6	0.9	8	14	2	7	31	1.9	61,176	8,775	444	537	70,932	7.1	0.3	(6.2)	(5.1)
Region VIII (Eastern Visayas)	26	3	1	–	30	1.6	400	17	1	–	418	60.3	105	2	–	1	108	6.7	28,324	2,355	70	40	30,789	3.1	(1.4)	57.2	3.7
Region IX (Zamboanga Peninsula)	25	3	1	2	31	1.7	10	2	–	–	12	1.7	176	14	–	–	190	11.8	30,888	2,216	73	67	33,244	3.3	(1.6)	(1.6)	8.5
Region X (Northern Mindanao)	133	34	1	–	168	9.2	1	–	–	1	2	0.3	13	2	1	–	16	1.0	33,040	4,079	155	138	37,412	3.7	5.5	(3.4)	(2.7)
Region XI (Davao Region)	21	8	1	1	31	1.7	4	–	1	–	5	0.7	10	1	–	1	12	0.7	52,449	5,758	252	226	58,685	5.9	(4.1)	(5.1)	(5.1)
Region XII (SOCCSKSARGEN)	23	6	–	2	31	1.7	1	–	–	–	1	0.1	121	6	–	–	127	7.9	41,581	3,121	120	118	44,940	4.5	(2.8)	(4.3)	3.4
Region XIII (Caraga)	22	3	–	–	25	1.4	2	–	–	–	2	0.3	22	6	1	1	29	1.8	18,069	1,687	67	50	19,873	2.0	(0.6)	(1.7)	(0.2)
Autonomous Region in Muslim Mindanao (ARMM)	1	–	–	–	1	0.1	1	–	–	–	1	0.1	–	–	–	–	–	–	7,730	423	14	9	8,176	0.8	(0.8)	(0.7)	(0.8)

ADB = Asian Development Bank; COVID-19 = coronavirus disease; MSME = micro, small, and medium-sized enterprise; PSA = Philippine Statistics Authority.

Sources: ADB Philippines MSME Surveys on COVID-19 Impact (March–April 2020, August–September 2020, and March–April 2021) and PSA List of Establishments 2018. Employment-based classification.

D. Thailand

Item	ADB Survey, March–April 2020 Employment Grouping						ADB Survey, August–September 2020 Employment Grouping						ADB Survey, March–April 2021 Employment Grouping						NSO 2017 Industrial Census Listing Employment Grouping						Difference between ADB and NSO Distribution (%)		
	Micro	Small	Medium	Large	Total	Share (%)	Micro	Small	Medium	Large	Total	Share (%)	Micro	Small	Medium	Large	Total	Share (%)	Micro	Small	Medium	Large	Total	Share (%)	March–April 2020	August–September 2020	March–April 2021
By industrial sector, total	696	425	44	15	1,180	100	351	158	17	6	532	100	487	420	73	13	993	100	2,243,638	229,891	15,121	4,396	2,493,046	100.0	–	–	–
Agriculture, forestry, and fishing	25	5	–	–	30	2.5	20	4	–	–	24	4.5	29	17	5	–	51	5.1	–	–	–	–	–	–	2.5	4.5	5.1
Mining and quarrying	–	–	–	–	–	–	–	–	–	–	–	–	2	–	1	–	3	0.3	–	–	–	–	–	–	–	–	0.3
Manufacturing	127	134	18	10	289	24.5	73	55	7	2	137	25.8	111	111	27	6	255	25.7	373,095	56,076	7,608	3,049	439,828	17.6	6.8	8.1	8.0
Electricity, gas, steam and air-conditioning supply	8	4	–	–	12	1.0	1	1	–	–	2	0.4	2	4	–	–	6	0.6	–	–	–	–	–	–	1.0	0.4	0.6
Water supply; sewerage, waste management and remediation activities	1	1	–	–	2	0.2	–	–	–	–	–	–	2	–	–	–	2	0.2	1,446	816	91	6	2,359	0.1	0.1	(0.1)	0.1
Construction	16	29	3	2	50	4.2	6	5	–	–	11	2.1	19	38	3	–	60	6.0	30,508	15,096	575	80	46,259	1.9	2.4	0.2	4.2
Wholesale and retail trade; repair of motor vehicles and motorcycles	301	108	16	1	426	36.1	40	5	1	–	46	8.6	118	101	14	3	236	23.8	1,043,453	85,928	3,453	469	1,133,303	45.5	(9.4)	(36.8)	(21.7)
Transport and storage	12	14	–	1	27	2.3	6	5	1	–	12	2.3	10	12	6	2	30	3.0	42,464	4,844	440	94	47,842	1.9	0.4	0.3	1.1
Accommodation and food service activities	49	23	4	–	76	6.4	31	21	1	–	53	10.0	36	25	3	1	65	6.5	311,789	36,645	1,357	210	350,001	14.0	(7.6)	(4.1)	(7.5)
Information and communication	31	23	1	–	55	4.7	8	3	1	1	13	2.4	23	20	1	–	44	4.4	10,019	2,334	203	33	12,589	0.5	4.2	1.9	3.9
Financial and insurance activities	2	5	–	–	7	0.6	–	–	–	–	–	–	–	2	1	–	3	0.3	–	–	–	–	–	–	0.6	–	0.3
Real estate activities	–	–	–	–	–	–	1	1	–	–	2	0.4	1	2	–	–	3	0.3	115,524	6,780	237	51	122,592	4.9	(4.9)	(4.5)	(4.6)
Professional, scientific, and technical activities	34	20	1	–	55	4.7	1	1	–	–	2	0.4	17	14	3	–	34	3.4	18,426	5,213	238	39	23,916	1.0	3.7	(0.6)	2.5
Administrative and support service activities	59	36	–	–	95	8.1	2	–	–	–	2	0.4	15	11	2	1	29	2.9	33,727	5,812	573	183	40,295	1.6	6.4	(1.2)	1.3
Public administration and defense; compulsory social security	–	–	–	–	–	–	–	–	–	–	–	–	–	–	–	–	–	–	–	–	–	–	–	–	–	–	–
Education	5	5	–	–	10	0.8	1	1	–	–	2	0.4	2	6	–	–	8	0.8	–	–	–	–	–	–	0.8	0.4	0.8
Human health and social work activities	18	14	–	1	33	2.8	3	1	–	–	4	0.8	4	1	–	–	5	0.5	1	62	101	139	303	0.0	2.8	0.7	0.5
Arts, entertainment, and recreation	3	–	–	–	3	0.3	1	1	–	–	2	0.4	10	2	–	–	13	1.3	24,960	4,193	164	37	29,354	1.2	(0.9)	(0.8)	0.1

Item	ADB Survey, March–April 2020 Employment Grouping						ADB Survey, August–September 2020 Employment Grouping						ADB Survey, March–April 2021 Employment Grouping						NSO 2017 Industrial Census Listing Employment Grouping						Difference between ADB and NSO Distribution (%)		
	Micro	Small	Medium	Large	Total	Share (%)	Micro	Small	Medium	Large	Total	Share (%)	Micro	Small	Medium	Large	Total	Share (%)	Micro	Small	Medium	Large	Total	Share (%)	March–April 2020	August–September 2020	March–April 2021
Other service activities	5	4	1	–	10	0.8	41	5	1	1	48	9.0	86	54	6	–	146	14.7	238,226	6,092	81	6	244,405	9.8	(9.0)	(0.8)	4.9
(Not identified)							116	49	5	2	172	32.3													–	32.3	–
By province, total	696	425	44	15	1,180	100.0	351	158	17	6	532	100.0	487	420	73	13	993	100.0	2,243,638	229,891	15,121	4,396	2,493,046	100.0	–	–	–
Amnat Charoen	3	1	–	–	4	0.3	2	–	–	–	2	0.4	2	–	–	–	2	0.2	10,825	724	18	–	11,568	0.5	(0.1)	(0.1)	(0.5)
Ang Thong	3	–	–	–	3	0.3	–	1	–	–	1	0.2	1	1	–	–	2	0.2	8,875	887	35	2	9,799	0.4	(0.1)	(0.2)	(0.2)
Bangkok	145	115	10	6	276	23.4	91	42	7	3	143	26.9	151	172	19	5	347	34.9	287,726	64,982	4,204	935	357,847	14.4	9.0	12.5	20.6
Bueng Kan	2	–	–	–	2	0.2	–	–	–	–	–	–	–	–	–	–	–	–	8,390	427	16	3	8,836	0.4	(0.2)	(0.4)	(0.4)
Buriram	7	3	–	–	10	0.8	3	1	1	–	5	0.9	3	–	–	–	3	0.3	39,497	1,767	94	7	41,365	1.7	(0.8)	(0.7)	(1.4)
Chachoengsao	4	3	–	1	8	0.7	2	1	–	–	3	0.6	4	5	2	–	11	1.1	18,113	3,129	499	210	21,951	0.9	(0.2)	(0.3)	0.2
Chai Nat	3	1	–	–	4	0.3	1	–	–	–	1	0.2	–	–	–	–	–	–	13,170	999	27	10	14,206	0.6	(0.2)	(0.4)	(0.6)
Chaiyaphum	2	1	1	–	4	0.3	1	–	–	–	1	0.2	3	1	–	–	4	0.4	27,673	1,460	45	9	29,187	1.2	(0.8)	(1.0)	(0.8)
Chanthaburi	6	1	–	1	8	0.7	3	2	–	–	5	0.9	2	3	–	–	5	0.5	14,832	1,227	42	5	16,106	0.6	0.0	0.3	(0.1)
Chiang Mai	45	24	–	1	70	5.9	29	7	–	–	36	6.8	29	13	3	1	46	4.6	74,419	8,247	298	59	83,023	3.3	2.6	3.4	1.3
Chiang Rai	15	11	–	–	26	2.2	6	3	–	–	9	1.7	9	1	–	–	10	1.0	48,379	4,153	88	5	52,625	2.1	0.1	(0.4)	(1.1)
Chonburi	22	13	1	–	36	3.1	9	4	1	–	14	2.6	15	11	4	–	30	3.0	55,493	9,075	805	433	65,806	2.6	0.4	0.0	0.4
Chumphon	3	2	–	–	5	0.4	2	1	–	–	3	0.6	2	2	–	–	4	0.4	18,097	1,353	64	17	19,531	0.8	(0.4)	(0.2)	(0.4)
Kalasin	7	2	–	–	9	0.8	4	–	–	–	4	0.8	5	–	2	–	7	0.7	38,010	1,851	57	7	39,925	1.6	(0.8)	(0.8)	(0.9)
Kamphaeng Phet	6	1	–	–	7	0.6	–	1	–	–	1	0.2	2	2	–	–	4	0.4	18,480	1,021	39	8	19,548	0.8	(0.2)	(0.6)	(0.4)
Kanchanaburi	5	2	–	–	7	0.6	5	1	–	–	6	1.1	4	4	–	–	8	0.8	26,351	1,777	99	18	28,245	1.1	(0.5)	0.0	(0.3)
Khon Kaen	11	8	1	–	20	1.7	7	7	–	–	14	2.6	10	6	–	–	16	1.6	57,381	3,272	100	28	60,781	2.4	(0.7)	0.2	(0.8)
Krabi	8	4	1	–	13	1.1	3	3	–	–	6	1.1	2	2	1	–	5	0.5	18,479	2,024	120	10	20,633	0.8	0.3	0.3	(0.3)
Lampang	10	5	–	–	15	1.3	5	2	1	–	8	1.5	5	3	–	–	8	0.8	27,720	2,129	74	20	29,943	1.2	0.1	0.3	(0.4)
Lamphun	5	4	–	–	9	0.8	4	–	1	–	5	0.9	3	1	1	–	5	0.5	20,132	1,308	75	54	21,569	0.9	(0.1)	0.1	(0.4)
Loei	6	–	–	–	6	0.5	2	–	–	–	2	0.4	1	1	–	–	2	0.2	13,076	854	9	2	13,941	0.6	(0.1)	(0.2)	(0.4)
Lopburi	4	1	–	–	5	0.4	3	–	–	–	3	0.6	2	2	–	–	4	0.4	22,330	1,804	89	26	24,249	1.0	(0.5)	(0.4)	(0.6)
Mae Hong Son	5	–	–	–	5	0.4	3	–	–	–	3	0.6	2	–	–	–	2	0.2	6,160	371	1	–	6,532	0.3	0.2	0.3	(0.1)
Maha Sarakham	3	–	–	–	3	0.3	2	–	–	–	2	0.4	1	2	–	–	3	0.3	38,558	2,094	48	6	40,706	1.6	(1.4)	(1.3)	(1.3)
Mukdahan	3	1	–	–	4	0.3	2	1	–	–	3	0.6	1	–	–	–	1	0.1	13,529	727	21	5	14,282	0.6	(0.2)	(0.0)	(0.5)
Nakhon Nayok	–	–	–	–	–	–	–	–	–	–	–	–	1	–	–	–	1	0.1	7,154	542	26	12	7,734	0.3	(0.3)	(0.3)	(0.2)
Nakhon Pathom	8	5	1	–	14	1.2	6	–	–	–	6	1.1	6	6	1	–	13	1.3	26,693	4,140	568	132	31,533	1.3	(0.1)	(0.1)	0.0
Nakhon Phanom	1	4	1	–	6	0.5	4	1	–	–	5	0.9	2	1	–	–	3	0.3	20,353	864	27	4	21,248	0.9	(0.3)	0.1	(0.6)
Nakhon Ratchasima	18	8	2	–	28	2.4	9	2	–	–	11	2.1	11	9	2	–	22	2.2	63,299	4,651	244	107	68,301	2.7	(0.4)	(0.7)	(0.5)
Nakhon Sawan	10	1	1	–	12	1.0	2	–	–	–	2	0.4	2	3	1	–	6	0.6	29,287	2,044	94	15	31,440	1.3	(0.2)	(0.9)	(0.7)

Item	ADB Survey, March–April 2020 Employment Grouping						ADB Survey, August–September 2020 Employment Grouping						ADB Survey, March–April 2021 Employment Grouping						NSO 2017 Industrial Census Listing Employment Grouping						Difference between ADB and NSO Distribution (%)		
	Micro	Small	Medium	Large	Total	Share (%)	Micro	Small	Medium	Large	Total	Share (%)	Micro	Small	Medium	Large	Total	Share (%)	Micro	Small	Medium	Large	Total	Share (%)	March–April 2020	August–September 2020	March–April 2021
Nakhon Si Thammarat	9	3	–	–	12	1.0	1	1	–	–	2	0.4	4	5	–	–	9	0.9	44,730	2,716	118	27	47,591	1.9	(0.9)	(1.5)	(1.0)
Nan	5	5	–	–	10	0.8	2	–	–	–	2	0.4	5	–	–	–	5	0.5	26,868	1,140	25	3	28,036	1.1	(0.3)	(0.7)	(0.6)
Narathiwat	3	3	–	–	6	0.5	1	–	–	–	1	0.2	–	–	–	–	–	–	20,569	835	25	2	21,431	0.9	(0.4)	(0.7)	(0.9)
Nong Bua Lamphu	2	1	–	–	3	0.3	–	–	–	–	–	–	1	2	1	–	4	0.4	14,084	615	30	2	14,731	0.6	(0.3)	(0.6)	(0.2)
Nong Khai	3	1	1	–	5	0.4	1	–	–	–	1	0.2	1	–	–	–	1	0.1	12,709	937	38	2	13,686	0.5	(0.1)	(0.4)	(0.4)
Nonthaburi	44	22	3	–	69	5.8	20	7	1	–	28	5.3	45	24	2	1	72	7.3	32,022	7,173	415	71	39,681	1.6	4.3	3.7	5.7
Pathum Thani	20	21	1	1	43	3.6	15	9	1	–	25	4.7	23	22	8	1	54	5.4	38,136	5,736	530	191	44,593	1.8	1.9	2.9	3.6
Pattani	8	4	–	–	12	1.0	3	2	1	–	6	1.1	4	2	–	–	6	0.6	15,562	875	30	7	16,474	0.7	0.4	0.5	(0.1)
Phang Nga	11	1	–	–	12	1.0	–	–	–	–	–	–	2	1	–	–	3	0.3	10,225	779	40	4	11,048	0.4	0.6	(0.4)	(0.1)
Phatthalung	6	2	–	–	8	0.7	2	2	–	–	4	0.8	2	1	–	–	3	0.3	25,109	1,260	20	1	26,390	1.1	(0.4)	(0.3)	(0.8)
Phayao	5	1	1	–	7	0.6	6	1	–	–	7	1.3	2	1	–	–	3	0.3	19,696	1,166	29	–	20,891	0.8	(0.2)	0.5	(0.5)
Phetchabun	4	–	–	–	4	0.3	2	1	–	–	3	0.6	1	1	–	–	2	0.2	25,462	1,676	41	10	27,189	1.1	(0.8)	(0.5)	(0.9)
Phetchaburi	5	6	–	–	11	0.9	1	1	–	–	2	0.4	1	4	–	–	5	0.5	17,169	1,616	76	23	18,884	0.8	0.2	(0.4)	(0.3)
Phichit	1	4	–	–	5	0.4	1	2	–	–	3	0.6	1	2	–	–	3	0.3	18,880	885	16	4	19,785	0.8	(0.4)	(0.2)	(0.5)
Phitsanulok	7	6	–	–	13	1.1	2	1	–	–	3	0.6	6	1	–	–	7	0.7	25,074	1,993	85	12	27,164	1.1	0.0	(0.5)	(0.4)
Phra Nakhon Si Ayutthaya	6	9	2	–	17	1.4	2	2	–	–	4	0.8	3	6	4	–	13	1.3	31,810	3,026	417	225	35,478	1.4	0.0	(0.7)	(0.1)
Phrae	10	1	–	–	11	0.9	2	1	–	–	3	0.6	1	1	–	–	2	0.2	38,555	1,414	21	2	39,992	1.6	(0.7)	(1.0)	(1.4)
Phuket	13	17	–	–	30	2.5	11	3	–	1	15	2.8	9	4	1	–	14	1.4	20,249	4,808	360	86	25,503	1.0	1.5	1.8	0.4
Prachinburi	4	4	–	–	8	0.7	2	2	–	–	4	0.8	1	1	–	–	2	0.2	17,777	1,032	121	103	19,033	0.8	(0.1)	(0.0)	(0.6)
Prachuap Khiri Khan	5	2	–	–	7	0.6	2	2	–	–	4	0.8	4	7	–	–	11	1.1	21,710	2,203	85	30	24,028	1.0	(0.4)	(0.2)	0.1
Ranong	1	–	–	–	1	0.1	–	–	–	–	–	–	2	–	–	–	2	0.2	7,879	851	33	14	8,777	0.4	(0.3)	(0.4)	(0.2)
Ratchaburi	8	8	3	–	19	1.6	3	2	1	–	6	1.1	10	8	4	1	23	2.3	26,293	2,776	207	68	29,344	1.2	0.4	(0.0)	1.1
Rayong	12	11	3	–	26	2.2	2	2	–	–	4	0.8	3	6	1	1	11	1.1	24,950	3,069	425	253	28,697	1.2	1.1	(0.4)	(0.0)
Roi Et	10	2	–	–	12	1.0	1	–	–	–	1	0.2	2	4	–	–	6	0.6	44,265	2,841	79	11	47,196	1.9	(0.9)	(1.7)	(1.3)
Sa Kaeo	2	1	–	–	3	0.3	–	–	–	–	–	–	3	–	–	–	3	0.3	20,941	1,046	22	6	22,015	0.9	(0.6)	(0.9)	(0.6)
Sakon Nakhon	–	1	1	–	2	0.2	5	–	–	–	5	0.9	1	1	–	–	2	0.2	27,286	1,029	40	4	28,359	1.1	(1.0)	(0.2)	(0.9)
Samut Prakan	17	16	3	2	38	3.2	14	8	–	1	23	4.3	17	22	5	1	45	4.5	44,677	7,922	1,337	446	54,382	2.2	1.0	2.1	2.4
Samut Sakhon	4	5	3	2	14	1.2	1	8	1	–	10	1.9	4	11	4	2	21	2.1	21,629	4,878	956	223	27,686	1.1	0.1	0.8	1.0
Samut Songkhram	3	1	–	–	4	0.3	–	1	–	–	1	0.2	2	1	–	–	3	0.3	5,439	806	43	10	6,298	0.3	0.1	(0.1)	0.0
Saraburi	2	7	–	–	9	0.8	4	2	–	–	6	1.1	2	1	1	–	4	0.4	17,802	1,969	192	131	20,094	0.8	(0.0)	0.3	(0.4)
Satun	3	–	–	–	3	0.3	–	–	–	–	–	–	2	2	–	–	4	0.4	11,407	721	25	3	12,156	0.5	(0.2)	(0.5)	(0.1)
Sing Buri	3	1	1	–	5	0.4	1	–	–	–	1	0.2	2	1	–	–	3	0.3	8,514	724	33	12	9,283	0.4	0.1	(0.2)	(0.1)
Sisaket	4	1	–	–	5	0.4	4	1	–	–	5	0.9	1	1	–	–	2	0.2	47,233	2,581	47	–	49,861	2.0	(1.6)	(1.1)	(1.8)

Item	ADB Survey, March–April 2020 Employment Grouping						ADB Survey, August–September 2020 Employment Grouping						ADB Survey, March–April 2021 Employment Grouping						NSO 2017 Industrial Census Listing Employment Grouping						Difference between ADB and NSO Distribution (%)		
	Micro	Small	Medium	Large	Total	Share (%)	Micro	Small	Medium	Large	Total	Share (%)	Micro	Small	Medium	Large	Total	Share (%)	Micro	Small	Medium	Large	Total	Share (%)	March–April 2020	August–September 2020	March–April 2021
Songkhla	15	7	–	–	22	1.9	11	4	–	–	15	2.8	12	5	3	–	20	2.0	45,804	3,836	267	97	50,004	2.0	(0.1)	0.8	0.0
Sukhothai	5	3	–	–	8	0.7	2	1	–	–	3	0.6	–	2	–	–	2	0.2	18,124	1,177	32	4	19,337	0.8	(0.1)	(0.2)	(0.6)
Suphan Buri	2	2	–	–	4	0.3	–	–	–	–	–	–	1	3	–	–	4	0.4	21,058	1,799	74	16	22,947	0.9	(0.6)	(0.9)	(0.5)
Surat Thani	13	4	1	–	18	1.5	5	1	–	–	6	1.1	8	3	1	–	12	1.2	46,677	4,326	235	35	51,273	2.1	(0.5)	(0.9)	(0.8)
Surin	6	1	1	–	8	0.7	1	1	–	–	2	0.4	4	2	–	–	6	0.6	65,608	2,527	63	8	68,206	2.7	(2.1)	(2.4)	(2.1)
Tak	10	2	1	–	13	1.1	–	3	–	–	3	0.6	2	3	–	–	5	0.5	15,078	1,480	90	19	16,667	0.7	0.4	(0.1)	(0.2)
Trang	3	6	–	–	9	0.8	4	1	–	–	5	0.9	3	2	–	–	5	0.5	29,111	1,713	81	25	30,930	1.2	(0.5)	(0.3)	(0.7)
Trat	3	2	–	–	5	0.4	1	–	–	–	1	0.2	–	1	–	–	1	0.1	7,100	686	39	6	7,831	0.3	0.1	(0.1)	(0.2)
Ubon Ratchathani	4	6	–	–	10	0.8	1	2	–	–	3	0.6	3	2	1	–	6	0.6	49,910	2,972	105	19	53,006	2.1	(1.3)	(1.6)	(1.5)
Udon Thani	10	1	1	–	12	1.0	4	–	–	–	4	0.8	4	3	–	–	7	0.7	36,060	2,683	136	20	38,899	1.6	(0.5)	(0.8)	(0.9)
Uthai Thani	3	1	–	–	4	0.3	1	–	–	–	1	0.2	–	–	–	–	–	–	10,149	660	21	1	10,831	0.4	(0.1)	(0.2)	(0.4)
Uttaradit	3	1	–	–	4	0.3	4	1	–	–	5	0.9	1	–	1	–	2	0.2	11,744	874	27	4	12,649	0.5	(0.2)	0.4	(0.3)
Yala	8	1	–	–	9	0.8	–	1	–	–	1	0.2	–	–	–	–	–	–	11,102	758	33	2	11,895	0.5	0.3	(0.3)	(0.5)
Yasothon	1	–	–	–	1	0.1	–	–	–	–	–	–	3	–	–	–	3	0.3	18,921	1,399	31	4	20,355	0.8	(0.7)	(0.8)	(0.5)

ADB = Asian Development Bank; COVID-19 = coronavirus disease; MSME = micro, small, and medium-sized enterprise; NSO = National Statistical Office.

Note: firms with 1–5 employees as microenterprises; firms with 6–50 employees as small enterprises; firms with 51–200 employees as medium-sized enterprises; and firms with 201 employees and above as large enterprises.

Sources: ADB Thailand MSME Surveys on COVID-19 Impact (March–April 2020, August–September 2020, and March–April 2021) and NSO 2017 Industrial Census Listing. Employment-based classification.

Appendix 2
Survey Response Counts

A. Indonesia

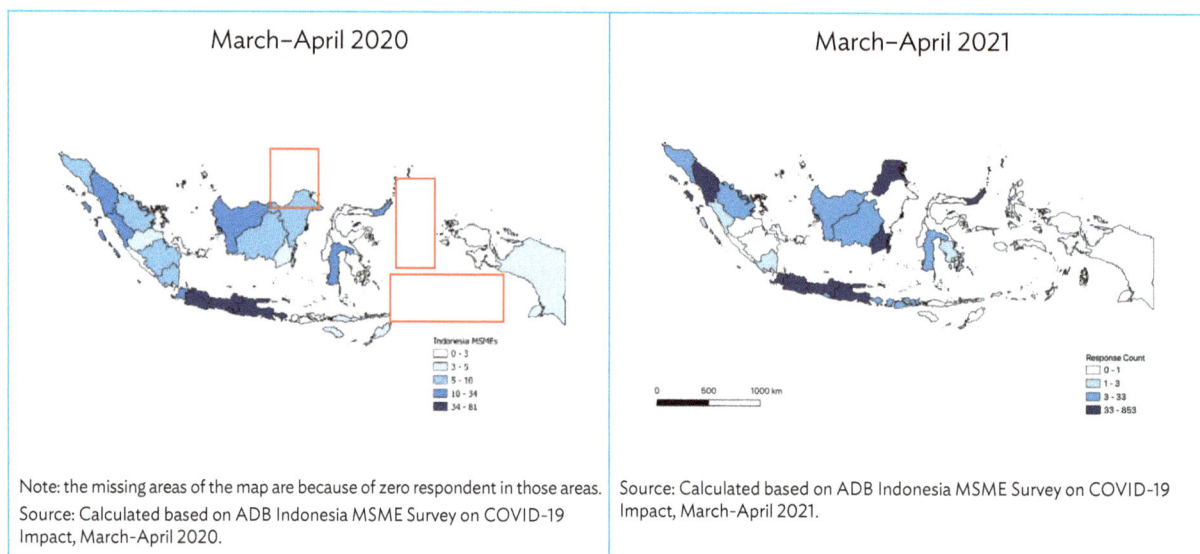

March–April 2020

March–April 2021

Indonesia MSMEs
- 0 - 3
- 3 - 5
- 5 - 10
- 10 - 34
- 34 - 81

Response Count
- 0 - 1
- 1 - 3
- 3 - 33
- 33 - 853

Note: the missing areas of the map are because of zero respondent in those areas.
Source: Calculated based on ADB Indonesia MSME Survey on COVID-19 Impact, March-April 2020.

Source: Calculated based on ADB Indonesia MSME Survey on COVID-19 Impact, March-April 2021.

B. Lao PDR

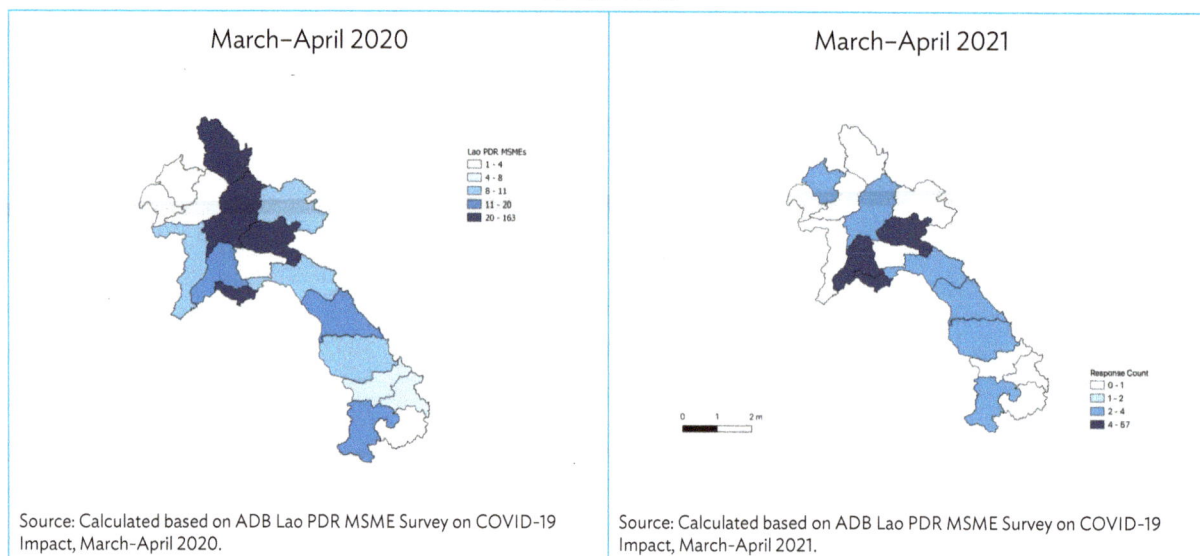

March–April 2020

March–April 2021

Lao PDR MSMEs
- 1 - 4
- 4 - 8
- 8 - 11
- 11 - 20
- 20 - 163

Response Count
- 0 - 1
- 1 - 2
- 2 - 4
- 4 - 57

Source: Calculated based on ADB Lao PDR MSME Survey on COVID-19 Impact, March-April 2020.

Source: Calculated based on ADB Lao PDR MSME Survey on COVID-19 Impact, March-April 2021.

C. Philippines

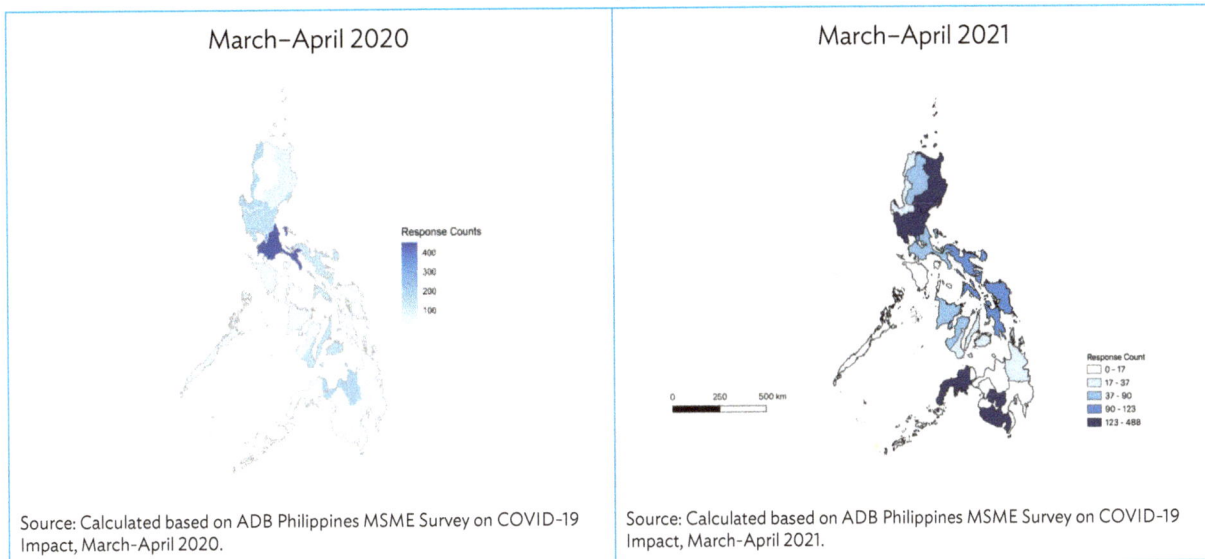

March–April 2020

Source: Calculated based on ADB Philippines MSME Survey on COVID-19 Impact, March-April 2020.

March–April 2021

Source: Calculated based on ADB Philippines MSME Survey on COVID-19 Impact, March-April 2021.

D. Thailand

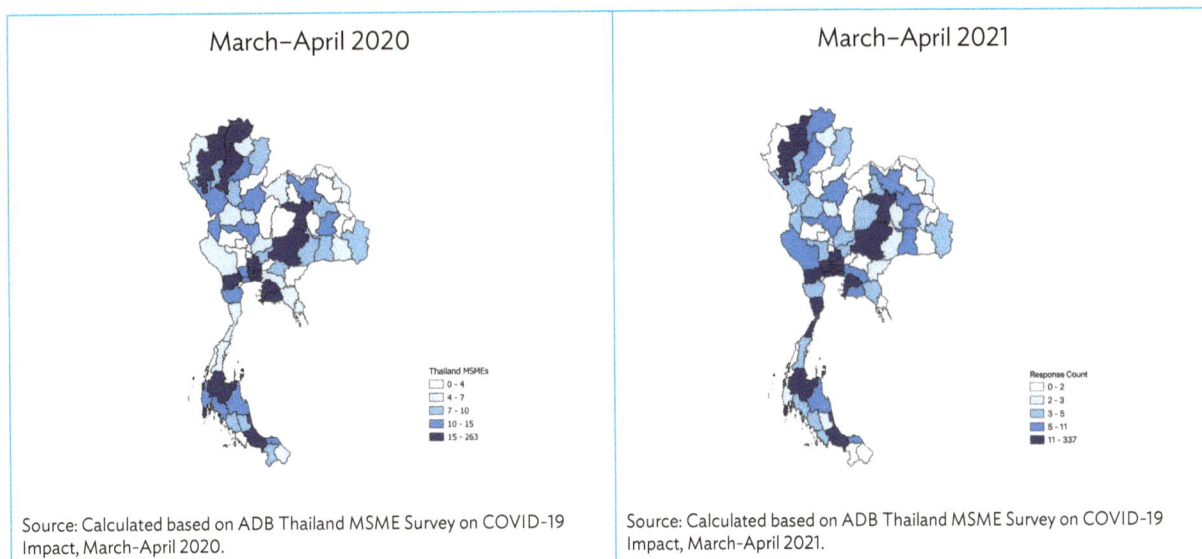

March–April 2020

Source: Calculated based on ADB Thailand MSME Survey on COVID-19 Impact, March-April 2020.

March–April 2021

Source: Calculated based on ADB Thailand MSME Survey on COVID-19 Impact, March-April 2021.